Bloodspurt:

The Films of Jean-Claude Van Damme

Edited by David C. Hayes

Bloodspurt: The Films of Jean-Claude Van Damme

This book is an independent work of research and commentary and is not sponsored, authorized or endorsed by, or otherwise affiliated with, any motion picture studio or production company affiliated with the films discussed herein. All uses of the name, image, and likeness of any individuals, and all copyrights and trademarks referenced in this book, are for editorial purposes and are pursuant of the Fair Use Doctrine.

The views and opinions of individuals quoted in this book do not necessarily reflect those of the author.

The promotional photographs and publicity materials reproduced herein are in the author's private collection (unless noted otherwise). These images date from the original release of the films and were released to media outlets for publicity purposes.

Published in the USA by
BearManor Media
1317 Edgewater Dr. #110
Orlando, FL 32804
www.BearManorMedia.com

Softcover Edition
ISBN-10:
ISBN-13: 979-8-88771-080-8

Printed in the United States of America

Dedicated in loving memory to Kevin Moyers.

Introduction

It was never my intention to start this introduction off by sounding like a stereotypical fan gushing over their favorite actor. But I have to apologize in advance because this is exactly what I am going to do. I thoroughly enjoy Jean-Claude Van Damme films. I have a sneaking suspicion that if you are reading this, then you do as well. It does not matter to me if you openly admit it or not. I am just glad you are here. For me, there is no secret. The action, the cheese, and the ridiculous scenarios that would never happen in real life (I'm looking at you, Frank Dux) is everything I want in a movie. Heck, my love for the Muscles from Brussels went so far that it inspired me to create a podcast about his filmography and life – Jean Pod Van Dammecast. In doing so, I have met new friends solely based off of a mutual love for Van Damme and his films. So, when I was asked if I would be willing to write this introduction to *Bloodspurt*, I had to jump at the opportunity.

Some may find it unbelievable or even humorous when they hear about my affection for JCVD, but the man holds a special place in my heart. The mere mention of his name brings a smile to my face as it is a constant reminder of all of the good times I had watching his films as a child. I cherish those cable television and VHS memories. It was no surprise for my mother to hear, "Anything with Van Damme," as a response to what movies we should rent from the video store.

Outside of my own adoration for JC, his Hollywood success story is enough to make anyone believe they can achieve their own goals if they have the right attitude and try hard enough. His story echoes the ideas of the American Dream. He is a real-life example of an immigrant success story. Like Arnold Schwarzenegger, he came to the U.S. seeking opportunity, and he found it. Any other man would have been content staying in Belgium as a gym owner after having a successful martial arts career. But Jean-Claude Van Varenberg dove headfirst into the land of screaming eagles and freedom to pursue his one goal – to become a movie star.

Like any human being, there are highs and lows associated with his life. He is known for his issues with infidelity, drug addiction, controversial friendships, and battling mental illness. However, Van Damme has shown over and over again throughout his career that anyone can overcome their demons if they fight hard enough. Whether or not you believe the stories of him doing helicopter kicks in front of producers, he has been able to continue to make a name for himself in the acting world. With more than seventy acting credits attached to his name, JCVD has still been able to keep his fame in the world of movies. Although some may believe he is past his glory years of starring in big blockbuster hits, Van Damme is still doing what he loves and using his platform to bring light to important issues.

Although he has been the butt of jokes in the French media regarding his political and philosophical views, no one can deny his love for animals. Even during the pandemic, Van Damme made national news once again by using his status to save a Chihuahua from being euthanized due to poor relations between Norway and Bulgaria. Love or hate him, he sticks to his guns and does whatever he can to fight for animal rights.

Do not even get me started on his acting. Yes, that is right, his acting. We all know him for his tropes and classic films, but throughout his career he continues to challenge himself. Though some reviewers may disagree with me on his later works, I am absolutely stunned that he still takes his job seriously rather than phoning it in for a paycheck. While he has nothing left to prove, he still seems to feel like he has everything left to prove. For instance, in his 2008 film, *JCVD*, Van Damme showed that he was meant for a serious role. He has also showcased his skills on the opposite side of the acting spectrum with the 2016 Amazon comedy series *Jean-Claude Van Johnson*. Even in 2019, he continued to challenge himself by accepting a role with no speaking parts in *We Die Young*.

Whether or not you agree with me about the actor himself, I hope that you get the same enjoyment in reading this book as I do in following his life. JCVD may have his flaws and his movies may not win any major film awards, but he continues to bring fans together from all over the world (Trust me, I'm in a few Facebook groups that confirm just that). I think that is a pretty great thing one man from Brussels can do.

- John Bruske

Woman in a Twilight Garden (1979), *Breakin'* (1984), *Missing in Action* (1984), & *Monaco Forever* (1984)

No, you did not accidentally pick up a book about Chuck Norris. Yes, Jean-Claude Van Damme DOES appear in Norris' seminal eighties action flick, *Missing in Action*. Well, sort of. I think. "Appear" is a strong word. He is listed in the stunt credits as J. Claude Van Damme, and as far as we know, the J stands for "Jean" and not "Jimmy" or "Jerry".

I looked for JCVD in *Missing in Action*. I did not find him. I turned it into a family game, a "Where's Waldo" of action movies, but none of my kids found him (they don't really know what he looks like, anyway, but I appreciate the effort). My wife DID find him…in an episode of *Friends*. Gah.

What we do know is that Jean-Claude IS in *Missing in Action*, and we know this because there exists an on-set photo of Van Damme dressed in army camouflage and flanked by two other, similarly dressed dudes.

Technically, *Missing in Action* is important in the annals of Van Damme history, and definitely noteworthy for being his first "action" role (as well as the Norris connection). It was a segue that led to his big breakthrough role as "Gay Karate Man" in *Monaco Forever*. Wait, no…it was one of the roles that led to his *eventual* big breakthrough role as Frank Dux in the immortal *Bloodsport*.

In my Herculean search to find proof of J. Claude's MIA appearance in, well, *MIA*, I did come across a video of a dual role in *Woman in a Twilight Garden*, a 1979 film set in Belgium and starring Rutger Hauer. Van Damme plays both "Movie Goer" and "Man in Garden" in a tour de force of a charismatic extra. Look it up on YouTube; six seconds of our hero sitting in a theater watching a movie (he does mention something quickly to the person sitting next to him), and a few more seconds as he sits in a garden and listens to others talk. He does take a rather convincing swig of a drink, but that's about it.

His next (uncredited) role is in the legendary 1984 flick *Breakin'*, and even though he again is only shown for a miniscule number of seconds, this is admittedly a pretty memorable scene. Because he is dancing and clapping while some break dancers, uh, break, and this is a *real* thing: people have accused him of trying to steal the scene with his over-the-top clapping. And if you give it a watch (and really, you should), you might think those people have a point. He is ripped, as well, and his exaggerated mountain-like handclaps do feel like an attempt to garner some extra attention.

But really, even though he is credited as Jean-Claude Vandam, the aforementioned part of "Gay Karate Man" in *Monaco Forever* is truly his first actual role, and he does quite well under the circumstances. He also gets to show off some of his martial arts moves, which are hilariously underlined with "woosh" sound effects. Gay Karate Man is driving, and he looks at the road for maybe 14 seconds of a 50 second drive, because he is coming onto his male passenger by way of rubbing his leg and asking him if he plays sports. No, really.

The dude gets angry and demands that Gay Karate Man get out of the car so he can "teach him a lesson in manners", to which Gay Karate Man pretends to be scared and even says, "Don't hurt me" as they walk to a fightin' area. After a particularly out of place slur for such a lighthearted scene (it was a different time), Van Damme peels off his weird robe shirt and shows off his ripped torso before launching into some beautiful roundhouse kicks (that he purposely doesn't connect with).

While the whole thing is SUPER silly, culminating in the passenger running away scared with the ol' Benny Hill-style fast edit, two things are fairly clear by the end of the scene:

1. Jean-Claude Van Damme (er, Vandam) is a pretty charismatic dude, and
2. Those kicks look like they could take someone OUT.

You can also find this scene streaming around online, and honestly, this is a must see if only for the unbelievable "what did I just watch" factor. It is a bit endearing despite all the strangeness.

So that accounts for three of his four earliest appearances…but how about *Missing in Action*? Well, the closest I could find to an actual scene is direct from JCVD's Instagram in a post commemorating the film and his work history with Chuck Norris (the two would both appear in 2012's *Expendables 2*). Here we have a clip from 1984 ofVan Damme holding up mats for Norris to punch and kick, which JC describes as "rare footage of me training Mr. Norris." Close enough, I suppose.

Van Damme would go onto bigger things only a couple years after *Monaco Forever* of course, scoring a role in eighties VHS stalwart *No Retreat, No Surrender.* That kickstarted his career in earnest and launched him into the world as a big action star, adored by men and women alike (including, eventually, Rachel Green and Monica Geller – more on that later).

Generally, an examination of a movie star's early career might lend some clues to their evolution, and even though we didn't really find "Waldo" in terms ofVan Damme's *Missing in Action* footage, we will always have Movie Goer, Spectator in First Dance Sequence, and Gay Karate Man to point to as the somehow glorious yet wholly inauspicious introduction to a truly memorable career.

- Paul Counelis

No Retreat, No Surrender (1986)

To write about this movie is to write about a selection of films I am most passionate about. It was the early '80s and Keith Strandberg had made contact with Hong Kong's Seasonal Films. A black belt in Isshinryu Karate, he was of course interested in action movies, and had already established himself as a writer for martial arts magazines. So he decided to find out if Seasonal might be interested in making a new sort of film, one that combined an American story, an American cast, with Hong Kong action.

Seasonal Films' owner Ng See Yuen was a visionary (he had started Jackie Chan's career) and he and Strandberg immediately hit it off. It didn't hurt that Strandberg also spoke Mandarin Chinese, and during that first afternoon they met for a long time, watching movies, talking about the future, and vowing to work together when he was ready to do an American movie.

That movie turned out to be *No Retreat No Surrender*, which we made in 1984 and was distributed in 1986, to outstanding success. It was one of the first American low budget martial arts films ever made, and it struck a chord with the audiences in theatres, as it had a wide theatrical release.

Back then, there was really no competition, and *NRNS* was made for very little money, shooting on location in LA and Seattle. The movie offered something few people had ever seen...Hong Kong-style action, done by Westerners. The movie was a huge hit and, as a result, Seasonal immediately started developing their next picture with Strandberg.

Over the next ten years the winning formula would continue until Seasonal's demise, but that decade of low-budget, action movie mayhem all began with *NRNS*. JCVD isn't in the majority of the flick, just in case you haven't seen it. Fashioned a little like a Karate Kid rip-off, Jason

Stillwell (Kurt McKinney, *ALF*) is a Bruce Lee freak who watches his Dad, Tom (Timothy D. Baker, *Angel of Destruction*), have the shit kicked out of him by JCVD, the Russian guy in the white suit that lets his fighting do the talking. Turns out the Mafia is buying up all the dojos around to use as fronts for their evil consortiums. Jason's Dad decides there's nothing else to do but leave. Thus, the family moves to Seattle and Jason immediately hooks up with his hetero life-mate R.J. (J.W. Falls, *Highway to Heaven*), a Michael Jackson-jazzy brother who has Jason's back before he ever has to ask.

Jason's neighborhood nemesis, Scott (Kent Lipham, *Bikini Summer*), is having his cake and eating it too when he decides to declare war on Stillwell. Mind you, he already has a running conflict with, as he puts it, "that slime-ball R.J." Scott has his reasons for the bad blood, but they are further tested when Jason goes against his dad's instructions and fights Scott and his burger-munching posse to save his friend. This leads to a series of arguments between father and son; fighting over that fact that fighting just gets you in more trouble. These backyard battles culminate with Tom Stillwell asserting his dominance and trashing Jason's Bruce Lee collection and makeshift dojo.

R.J. helps Jason take all his 'useless junk', as his father labels it, to a squat in the middle of the night...and that's when things turn magical. There have been many incarnations of the benevolent benefactor; the ancient and wise teacher who helps transforming the scrawny weakling in a martial arts master. Who better to show up and answer Jason's cries for help...than the ghost of Bruce Lee! That's right. I'll say it again because it's cool to ponder; Jason is helped to rise to the seat of martial arts glory, defeat bad Russian JCVD, get the girl and save Seattle karate from being swallowed by the evil mafia bosses...by the ghost...of Bruce Lee!

"Lee Dai Goh, you call me. Shall we begin?" These are some of the first words of the legendary dragon, doomed like Hamlet's father for a certain term to walk the earth until Jason gets his montages done. Bruce's ghost is played appropriately by Tae-jeong Kim, who at one time in history stood in for the man himself. Lee Dai Goh or Big Brother Lee trains Jason up. He's watched his father be suppressed into a coward, had his head kicked in by his girlfriend's jealous wannabe lover and his Bruce Lee posters ripped to shreds. Now is the time, and with the spectral Bruce to show Jason the way, he hooks back up with his girl at a disco, shows his Dad that sometimes you just *have* to fight and finally, with ten minutes till the credits roll, JCVD makes his reappearance only to find he forgets how to kill when Jason, red tracksuit and all, has the balls to get into the ring and end the evil Russian's psychological hold on his future with the devastating finishing move, handed down to him...by a legend.

The *No Retreat, No Surrender* series would continue, but McKinney and Van Damme didn't want to go to Thailand at the time. So, Loren Avedon (*King of the Kickboxers*) would take the lead, while JCVD would be replaced by Matthias Hues (*I Come in Peace* aka *Dark Angel*) for *Raging Thunder, NRNS 2*. But that's another story…

- Kent Hill

Bloodsport (1988)

Donald Gibb is really the only reason to watch this movie. Dude really makes you fall in love with him enough, so when Bolo at last tries to crack his skull open, one is motivated enough to persist through JCVD, making all sorts of funny noises (and faces), till at last the kid is back in the picture, sucking down cold brewskies in a shitty Hong Kong hospital.

Okay...maybe there is a little more to it than that. First off, it's a Cannon movie, so, right away, you kind of know what you're in for. Frank Dux (and you really should read into this guy) is a real dude whose life this movie is based on. But, depending on what you read you'll discover, a piece at a time, is it's mostly bullshit. His exploits are like an 80's medium-budget action movie version of the documentary *Kung Fu Elliot* (you should check that out too).

So JCVD plays Dux...once he gets over those difficult teenage years. See young Frank gets caught trying to steal a Katana sword. "Nice try, Lao Che," and young Frank is not getting off the hook so easily for is attempt at petty larceny just to fit in with the cool kids. He is busted by the Katana's owner Tanaka (Roy Chiao, *Indian Jones ant the Temple of Doom*). Tanaka agrees to let Frank earn his penance by helping Tanaka train his son Shingo (Sean Ward, *The Sean Ward Show*), so that he may one day represent the Tanaka clan at the Kumite, a back-alley tournament in Hong Kong where fighters occasionally get killed...so you better have the balls to get into the ring.

Shingo unfortunately dies before he gets a chance to get killed at the Kumite so Dux, now JCVD, asks Tanaka to train him. Tanaka is not hip to the idea because JCVD is not a Tanaka...but...it's going to throw a spanner in the works if dude doesn't get a training montage that we can cut back to at pivotal moments during the final fight sequence of the big showdown... so for cinematic symmetry, Tanaka relents. He even teaches how to catch fish with lighting speed, which also pays off later.

We get all this courtesy of flashbacks when Frank goes to visit the dying Tanaka just before he heads for Hong Kong. Apparently, Frank is too valuable to just go off a get killed in the Kumite, so a couple a fun-loving CIC foils are sent to arrest him and stop him from honouring his Shidoshi. These are Helmer and Rawlins played respectively by Norman Burton (*American Ninja 5*) and future Oscar winner, Forest Whitaker (*Platoon*).

Frank makes it to the hotel on time to hook up and play video games with our boy Ray Jackson (Donald Gibb, *Revenge of the Nerds*) and eventually meet tour guide Victor Lin (Ken Siu, *Off Limits*). Lin after calling Frank Ducks, takes them to sign up for the fights. Problem is the local boys don't buy JCVD as a member of the Tanaka Clan, so he has to use the tried-and-true Dim Mak, to break one brick at the bottom of a pile, to prove he knows what he's talking about.

"Very good. But brick not hit back!" as Chong Li (Bolo Yeung, *Enter the Dragon*) says in the wake of JCVD's flaunting of his prowess. Thus, the Kumite is on. Everyone gets together for a series of shots showing different opponents and their alternative styles of hand-to-hand combat. That is...until it's time for Frank to put up his dukes. "His first fight of the Kumite and he broke the fucking world record!" cries Ray Jackson as JCVD gets off to a soaring start.

He allows himself few distractions during the comp, aside from chasing Janice Kent's (Leah Ayres, *All That Jazz*) tail, getting himself a little love whilst outrunning Forest and Norman, those wily CIC agents who have called in the help of the Hong Kong police. Captain Chen (Philip Chan, who you'll see is still out to get JCVD in *Double Impact*) and his force are no match for a raging Van Damme, who doesn't really give a Van Damme about anything by this point. You see Bolo has seriously fucked our boy Jackson up, nearly killed the cat, so JCVD now is out for not only revenge, but he is still trying to be the best he can be...for himself...for Jackson...and his Shidoshi too. Janice says she is not going to sit around and watch Frank get killed, but she seems happy once again to pose as a female escort to slink her way into the Kumite to see just that.

At last, we arrive at the big fight. Chong and Frank have bested the rest, now it's time to bring all that emotion, history, flashbacks, funny faces, equally funny noises, slow-motion strikes and the obligatory moments were JCVD looks like he's about to lose just so the crowd can get behind him, just so the film can rise to the crescendo, and Van Damme can finally earn that Katana sword he was looking to steal back in the day...just so he could fit in with the cool kids.

Like you may have guessed, JCVD wins, Jackson is lucky his head is as hard as a brick, Janice gets to do JCVD's little *salute* to him after he shares a final friendly "fuck you" with Forest and Norman before he jumps a plain back to the world over a title card that tells you everything you've just seen is true. Of course...if you read a little more on the real Frank Dux, you'll find that there's a reason his *true* story, made a perfect Cannon vehicle for their *new* cocky and coked-up Michael Dudikoff.

- Kent Hill

Black Eagle (1988)

Let's Leave it All

After Jean-Claude Van Damme in *Black Eagle* (1988)

Andrei, let's leave it all.
Have you seen Malta this time of year?
Temple ruins, mosaics, patina-green wharfs,
Chianti, and cantaloupe-colored skies.
I'd sail us toward a horizon we'd never catch.

If you had been a persuadable man,
I would've crafted a more compelling argument.

You were ridiculous when I first saw you on my ship,
not just throwing knives with marksman precision,
but hurling blades while in the splits atop oil drums.

Who does that? You're a bad boy Ken doll, or
an 80s action figure. Black hair slicked back,
painted-on clothing, and dislocated femurs.

Would you have ever been content wandering
museums, or regaling dinner party guests
with your quips, the ones you spat to enemies
after stoically wiping blood from your mouth?

You were an olive and fig daydream,
loyal to a country that didn't care
if you lived or died—
    and you did die, bullet to the leg,
    swallowed by propeller-whirled waves.

- Justine Defever

Black Eagle is one of those 80s movies that definitely was trying to make money off of the Cold War. It cuts to the chase as it starts out with an F-111 being shot down over Malta by Russians that was carrying a very important package – an experimental top secret laser guidance system. It's now up to the U.S. to retrieve the device before the Russians get to it. There's only one man for the job – Ken Tani (played by Sho Kosugi). The antagonist, Colonel Vladimir Klimenko, leads a band of KGB agents, including the ever so charming and intimidating Andrei, played by none other than a young Jean-Claude Van Damme.

The film begins with an awkward loud voice over of the plane crashing during open shots of the U.S. trying to set up a recovery mission in Malta. The U.S. brass determines they need Black Eagle, aka Ken Tani, but he's currently on another mission and is heading for his two-week vacation to spend time with his sons. But there's a change of plans when the kids are led to Malta by CIA agent Patricia Parker.

One agent is anxious to go retrieve the system by himself and won't wait for Ken to arrive. Obviously, this is a huge mistake as he ends up getting caught, questioned, and ultimately killed by Van Damme after trying to fight off the Russians. Ken finally makes his way to Malta after finding out that his kids are there waiting for him. He makes a fantastic entrance – he skydives out of an unidentified plane and into the ocean. He comes in undercover and meets up with his kids and Patricia. Meanwhile, JC is doing his patented splits on some oil drums while throwing knives, impressing his Russian love interest.

The Colonel knows something is up with Ken – they can't find any information on him, but they are able to pinpoint everyone else around him. They are unsuccessful in trying to capture him. Later in the evening, Ken goes undercover with Patricia at a casino but it's too late. The Colonel is there, and he lets them both know that he's onto them. As they return to their rooms, Ken notices someone is waiting for him. He busts through the back door and knocks the guy out, following up with getting his kids and everyone else out of there and into a new, safe location.

The Colonel has been tasked with putting the laser system on a freighter. However, Ken gets to the system first on his paraglider and glides his way over to the crash, where he jumps off and dives into the water. After a small confrontation, Ken is able to give the goods to the head U.S. guy. But it's not over – the boss tells Ken he needs to take out the Colonel and then he can get his two weeks off. Ken says he'll do it under one condition – get his kids out of Malta safely. The boss agrees.

But plans don't go accordingly as Van Damme is tailing the car containing the kids and Patricia. A car chase pursues but they are ultimately caught when the driver reveals he's been a double agent all along. As they are all being taken away, one of Ken's kids escapes. He doesn't get too far when he gets jumped by a bunch of other kids until the police show up. Lucky for Ken, he is able to get his son after some questioning from the head Inspector.

After searching, he locates his other son and Patricia based off her fast action of taking the son's baseball cap and hanging it on the side of the building they are occupying. Ken goes on a serious beat down rescue quest as he snaps one guy's neck, throws another guy off a building, and makes another stab himself with his own knife. The kids and Patricia are able to get away, but Van Damme stops Ken. They have a great back and forth fight with what appears to be JC getting the upper hand, until Ken points at him and jumps off a cliff and into the water to escape.

Ken is now meeting up with one of the other agents as they go undercover to get on the Colonel's freighter. They are able to plant a device that deactivates the navigational system. As night falls, Ken puts on his war paint while JC is with his love interest in bed.

Things get intense as the fighting begins. They plant the bombs, Ken fights JC in another back-and-forth match with Ken finally getting the upper hand. Here's where things get weird – the other agent shoots JC in the leg. Jean-Claude then hobbles off the dock and into the water. He tells his love interest to jump in after him, which she does. Then the boat starts up and the force of the propellers sucks JCVD into it, killing him instantly. It was a very weird and random death that apparently needed to happen with only a few minutes of the film left.

Ken then takes out the Colonel and jumps off the boat with his agent friend as the boat explodes. They get back on the dock and see the Inspector that questioned Ken earlier, who politely tells him to leave Malta. He does so and meets up with his kids and Patricia elsewhere. The movie fades out.

This is a pretty tame movie for the era. It's not too memorable, even with JC playing the role of a bad guy. It has an interesting story but not interesting enough to hold attention. Even if JC were to reverse roles, it still wouldn't be as good as some of his other films. The secondary story of Ken's kids not being able to see their father is what really captured me. These were Sho Kosugi's real kids, and while the acting wasn't the greatest, they at least had the ability to be a part of a film with their father. I'm sure there were parallels in real life to dealing with their father's busy schedule. Outside of that, this movie is really only for the hardcore 80s action and Van Damme fans. Otherwise, it can stay in the past.

- John Bruske

Cyborg (1989)

Auteur theory is bullshit.

There, I said it.

Do you love Alfred Hitchcock's tense, twisty-turny plots and slow-building psychological suspense? Maybe what you really love are the screenplays of John Michael Hayes, Ernest Lehman, Joan Harrison, and Whitfield Cook.

Do you love Ridley Scott's sleek, biomechanical monsters and neon-lit, cyberpunk cityscapes? Maybe what you really love are the art designs of H.R. Giger and Syd Mead.

More than any other medium, save for video games, cinema is a profoundly collaborative art form. With hundreds if not thousands of creators contributing to a single project, including actors, editors, cinematographers, and more, the idea that *any* director could ever be credited with primary authorship of *any* picture is, well, bullshit.

Case in point: 1989's *Cyborg*.

A low-budget sci-fi schlocker from Cannon Films, *Cyborg* sees a young Jean-Claude Van Damme in his second ever starring role as Gibson Rickenbacker, a stoic, mercenary "Slinger" karate-kicking his way through a plague-ridden, post-apocalyptic future.

Gibson is hunting down the Flesh Pirates, a sadistic gang of cannibals who murdered the woman he loved. Along the way he crosses paths with Pearl Prophet, the titular cyborg whose robo-head contains data about a potential cure for the gruesome disease known as Living Death. When Pearl herself ends up in the clutches of the Flesh Pirates, it's up to Gibson to rescue her and finally slay Fender Tremolo, the group's hulking leader, who wants the cure for his own poorly defined but clearly devious ends.

Gibson Rickenbacker? Pearl Prophet? Fender Tremolo? Yes, those really are the character's names. And, yes, they're all named after musical instrument manufacturers. You can thank writer-director Albert Pyun for that.

What you can't thank him for is the casting of the film's hero. Pyun originally wanted Chuck Norris to play the lead, but producers Menahem Golan and Yoram Globus insisted on Van Damme. In a twist of fate, this substitution would ultimately save *Cyborg* in its darkest hour.

Surely, you've heard of Workprint Cuts and Director's Cuts. If you follow the ups and downs of the *Halloween* franchise, you've even heard of Producer's Cuts. But how often have you heard of a film having an Actor's Cut? Well, that's exactly what the theatrically released version of *Cyborg* is.

See, when Van Damme viewed Pyun's final cut, alarm bells went off. The ambitious martial artist-turned-actor could see his chances of Hollywood stardom blowing away like a fart in the wind. So, just like *Bloodsport* before it, Van Damme convinced Golan and Globus to let him personally reedit *Cyborg*.

The result?

Before Van Damme's recut, test audiences uniformly panned the film. Hardly surprising given how hastily it'd been cobbled together using pre-production elements left over from a cancelled Spider-Man adaptation and *Masters of the Universe* sequel. Following the recut, though, *Cyborg* earned a U.S. box office of more than $10 million against a budget of $500,000. It made even more money on VHS. Most importantly, it helped cement Van Damme as a bona fide action-movie icon.

Despite *Cyborg*'s success, Pyun was understandably less than thrilled. What he'd intended as a dark, theological war opera had been transformed into a solid but straightforward revenge yarn. Come 2011, Pyun decided to reassemble his original cut using footage culled from old video tapes, releasing it on his own so that audiences could finally see his true auteur vision.

Watching Pyun's cut, the first alteration you'll likely notice is that the central plot MacGuffin is completely different. Instead of curing a plague, Pearl Prophet's bizarrely vague goal is now to bring back "technology" (weird considering how guns, boats, and, oh yeah, *cyborgs* are all shown to exist). Fender Tremolo's once similarly vague goal, meanwhile, is now clarified: he wants to create a literal "Hell on Earth" because he's, um, a devil-worshiper.

Yes, really.

The other major change comes in the form of an expanded denouement wherein Pearl's motivations are revealed to be less than virtuous (thus deflating the film's hard-earned sense of climactic triumph). Afterward, in a newly filmed epilogue, Pyun homages *The Terminator* by having a naked cyborg appear inside a crackling ball of light, in what is ostensibly a tie-in for the director's yet unreleased follow-up, *Cyborg Nemesis: The Dark Rift*.

Admittedly, the cut of *Cyborg* released to theaters is far from a masterpiece. It's cheesy and poorly acted, and it overuses slow-motion to a degree that would make even Zack Snyder groan. But it's also fast-paced, hard-hitting, and ghoulishly fun. The fight scenes, sets, special effects, matte paintings, and cinematography are all exceptional, and Van Damme brings a piercing intensity that helps sell the hoary hokum that surrounds him.

In contrast, the Director's Cut is longer and slower, but not any grander or smarter. There's more dialogue, but it's as perfunctory in its construction as it is in its delivery. The characters are better explained, but they're also *over*-explained and, in the case of both Pearl and Fender, the explanations given are so off-putting that having no explanation at all would be preferable.

The only real improvements the Director's Cut makes are a few small restorations of deleted gore and the replacement of Kevin Bassinson's cheap-sounding synth score with a more dramatic, guitar-driven one by Tony Riparetti and Jim Saad.

Just like with George Lucas, the lesson here is that a "director's preferred version" isn't always superior. In fact, sometimes a director is the person who understands the appeal of value of their own work the least.

That said, Pyun is not a bad director, despite what some critics say. Unorthodox? Yes. Idiosyncratic? Definitely. When his idiosyncrasies mesh together just right with those of his collaborators, though, you get charming cult oddities like *Dollman*, *Radioactive Dreams*, *Vicious Lips*, and *The Sword and the Sorcerer.* When they don't, you get tiresome misfires like *Alien from L.A.* and *Omega Doom.*

Without Van Damme, *Cyborg* would've ended up a lot closer to the latter than the former. Say what you will about the man's skills as an actor, but it seems he's actually a damn good editor.

Good thing Pyun didn't cast Chuck Norris instead.

- William Tea

Kickboxer (1989)

The year is 1989. Van Damme is fresh off of his successful run with *Bloodsport* and he's starting to become popular in the eyes of many movie goers. What better way to showcase his talent and ability than by putting him in another fighting film? This time, Van Damme has to learn the ancient martial art of Muay Thai!

Arguably, *Kickboxer* is one of JCVD's most popular films. I remember asking a group of friends, "What movie comes to mind when you think of Jean-Claude Van Damme?" A third of them had replied with Kickboxer. While the movie may have been seen as another action film distributed by Cannon, there was no denying that it had a pretty successful run at the box office and would go on to spawn four sequels.

We're met with two brothers – Kurt and Eric Sloane. As the older Eric is making his name known in the world of kickboxing, Kurt is his corner man trying to live life to the fullest. After becoming the best in the U.S., Eric decides he needs to go worldwide with his fighting. We can tell this is his first mistake when he doesn't even know the difference between Taiwan and Thailand.

Kickboxer is a movie full of montages. This should come as no surprise because pretty much every action film back then was full of them. The Sloane brothers find themselves adventuring into Thailand; and it is exactly what you picture when you think of Thailand in the 1980s. "Streets of Siam" plays on as the Sloane brothers take in the view of Bangkok. After the boat ride and a hilarious exchange in which Eric tells Kurt that a lady wants to "make it with the champ," things begin to get serious as Eric prepares to face off against Tong Po.

Eric was played by the real-life Undisputed Heavyweight Kickboxing Champion, Dennis Alexio. While Alexio may have been able to stand up against Tong Po in real life, his character Eric bites off more than he can chew. Let me tell you about Tong Po. Michel Qissi, the childhood friend of Van Damme, plays one of the scariest antagonists I have ever seen in a film. Forget Freddy and Jason. As a kid, I remember being deathly afraid of Tong Po. His stance, his style, the mean look on his face – nothing seemed to break him. I knew my fear of this monster was confirmed when even Van Damme was scared seeing Tong Po kicking a concrete pillar while pieces of plaster fell all around him.

Worried for his brother, Kurt tries to convince Eric not to take the fight. This is Eric's second mistake, as he feels he has to prove himself. As a viewer, we know where this is going. He doesn't so much prove himself as he proves that Tong Po is a bad dude. Eric gets beaten close to death as Van Damme tries to intervene, but it's all for nothing. Tong Po delivers a devastating elbow to Eric's back that leaves him paralyzed below the waist. I know the critics were harsh on JCVD when this film came out, but I was surprised to see his acting ability when finding out the news about his brother. His tears seemed real.

Coincidentally, Van Damme meets Winston Taylor, an ex-special forces soldier that helps get Eric to the hospital. Obviously, Van Damme is livid about the whole thing so he does the only thing any brother would do in a situation like this – he has to train to get his revenge. Welcome to the wonderful world of Cannon as more montages complete the film. Van Damme meets up with one of the greatest teachers, Xian Chow, to learn all about Muay Thai. It's these times where the movie really shines – I couldn't help but laugh as I watched Van Damme try to improve his cardio by having meat tied to him so that a dog could chase after him. He kicks a palm tree to toughen up his shins, but it seems like a losing battle as he speaks out to Xian Chow, "You want me to break my leg?" Of course, I also have to mention one of the greatest scenes of all time in cinematic history – Van Damme drunkenly dancing with women while fighting guys that were convinced he was talking about their mothers having sex with mules. Needless to say, this movie is as ridiculous as it sounds. But I mean that in the absolute best way.

After more training scenes, we're at the final fight – this time it's an underground Muay Thai fight. It's a battle to see who the best is as both men wear next to nothing while having their hemp rope wrapped hands dipped in resin and glass shards. It has all come down to this moment, and wouldn't you know it? Due to all of his training, Kurt becomes an even better fighter than his world champion brother. Van Damme ultimately beats Tong Po and avenges his brother. Oh, did I forget to mention that bad guys kidnapped Eric, Tong Po raped Xian's niece, and Kurt was supposed to throw the fight? Yes, this film is absolute madness. But of course, with the help of Winston, they are able to save everyone, and Kurt is able to beat Tong Po while the crowd chants "Nuk Soo Kow." Happy ending, right?

While I absolutely love this film, there are many scenes and action sequences that could only have been done in the 1980s and should rightfully be left in that time period. I'm sure people in Thailand weren't too happy with how some things were portrayed but then again, this film felt like it was a 90-minute commercial for a Bangkok tourist destination. I know for a fact this movie has convinced other children from the 80s to go over to Thailand to visit and train.

I love talking about certain Van Damme tropes that always appear in his movies. Of course, the first one everyone thinks about is the splits. The second is shots to the groin. There are other tropes, including headbutting, yelling, or screaming "No," but I don't need to mention those ones. You better believe we got to see some split action in this film. The last time I counted, there were four different times where the splits made an appearance.

In the grand scheme of things, this may not be a movie for everyone. But as a kid in the late 80s, the censored version on TBS had everything I needed. Sure, I enjoyed watching Stallone and Arnie tear it up but give me Van Damme doing the splits and kicking ass any day.

- John Bruske

Lionheart (1990)

Lionheart is the 1990 Jean-Claude Van Damme movie about street fighting. Van Damme's Lyon Gaultier leaves his French Foreign Legion post to visit his brother, Francois, after Francois was brutally beaten and burned in a drug deal gone bad.

Lyon learns the hard way that the streets of the United States aren't as friendly as they appear. He has to join underground street fighting fights to earn money to travel from New York to Los Angeles.

It's not a pretty picture. But Lyon gets the job done.

Something I enjoyed about *Lionheart* was the leadership lessons you could find in the movie. We're going to look at the leadership lessons I took away and how they can make you a better leader.

Leadership Lessons from *Lionheart*

1. Do what needs to be done:

Mail was being delivered to Lyon but the two mail carriers wouldn't hand over the letter. They liked how the envelope smelled of perfume. They continued to play keep away. Lyon was done. He wanted his letter. He stabbed the letter with his knife to get it. Leaders do what needs to be done (within the confines of what is right). They go above and beyond to get the job done. What are you willing to do to lead well? Do it.

2. Use the resources around you:

Lyon was going to head to the United States against his commanding officer's orders. This gave him a trip to the sweatbox. Once there, Lyon wouldn't go into the sweatbox. He fought back. He used the resources around him to fight back. He broke a pole holding up a net and used the pole as a weapon. He found an ammo container to hit one of his attackers. He used the resources around him to fight. You can use the resources around you as well. There are more resources available to you than you realize. Just look around. See what you can use to get the job done. You will be surprised.

3. Attitude is okay:

Cynthia was a fight promoter. Lyon gave her attitude when she wanted to know more about him. She was okay with the attitude... as long as Lyon performed. You will hire people who may have an attitude. These people may be able to get the job done. That's what matters. Be willing to deal with a little bit of attitude if they get the job done.

4. Bad leaders bet against their talent:

Cynthia had a fighter named Sonny. He was one of her best. Once she met Lyon, she defected. She chose to begin to bet against her fighter and on Lyon instead. This was a defection. A breach of trust. That's what betting against your talent does. It says you don't trust them. Beware of betting against your talent.

5. Joshua became Lyon's manager in New York. He traveled with him to Los Angeles.

While there, he had Cynthia put them up in a fancy, dandy hotel. Joshua told Lyon it is nice to have friends. It is nice to have friends. Friends in leadership means your influence will go further than it could with only you behind it. Make sure you're making friends in business. They will help you get further than you could on your own.

6. Leadership takes time:

Sgt. Hartog and Moustafa had been sent by the French Foreign Legion to track down Lyon. They wanted him back after he defected and left for the United States. The duo staked out Lyon's sister-in-law Helene's apartment to see if he would show up. It took a long time, but Lyon was finally spotted. They were right in where they were looking. Leaders can get tired of waiting. They think it is a waste of time if something isn't happening. That's not true. Leadership takes time. You will have to wait. You will have to hunker in place. But, when the time is right, the wait is worth it.

7. Bad leaders think only about money:

Cynthia discovered Lyon had setup a fake bank account as an insurance agency. The money in this account was going to Helene. This set Cynthia off. She thought Lyon was sleeping with Helene. This wouldn't have been a huge problem except Cynthia was scared the money would stop flowing to her. She wanted to make sure Lyon would continue to fight. This is bad leadership 101. Cynthia was concerned with the money. She wasn't concerned about the person. All she wanted was the flow of money to continue. Leaders need to stop being concerned about the money. Money is important, yes... But it is not the most important thing. Your people are the most important. Make sure they're taken care of. If you do this, the money will continue to flow.

8. Don't lose your heart:

Joshua told Lyon he had a big heart. It was great to see. It was also dangerous. Later, Joshua changed his tune. He told Lyon "Don't ever lose it because you'll never get it back." Joshua realized how important a big heart was. Having a big heart in leadership can be tough. Your heart is constantly hurt. It is constantly challenge. Yet, if you keep a big heart, you are able to continually help people. You are able to find new ways to do business. Your heart is your biggest asset in leadership. Listen to Joshua. Don't lose your heart. If you do, you will struggle to get it back. Keep your big heart. It is worth it.

- Joe LaLonde

Death Warrant (1990)

Out of all the action stars to come out during the golden era of action cinema, mainly the 80's and 90's, one, to me any way, stood out from the Seagals and Norrises of the world: Jean-Claude Van Damme.

While most of his films are your standard fight fest, with the usual plot (revenge being the key plot point) of the main star, in this case Van Damme, facing off against the main antagonist in the finale. You know, hero's brother/friend/mentor gets murdered, he seeks out those that were involved (usually gangsters or some criminal empire), gets his ass whooped, comes back in the end and disposes of said bad guys. Van Damme was different in the sense that some of his work was unique: *Time Cop, Universal Soldier, Cyborg*, and in one of his later films, and surely a film where you can see how Mr. Van Damme has matured, in a wink-wink, meta kind of way, *JCVD*. I didn't say his movies are Cannes-worthy, but some are fun romps with a shit ton of spinning kicks and glorious violence.

Then there is *Death Warrant*. A film released in 1990, during the height of home video rentals and Friday night trips to Blockbuster, and most surely would be stacked next to other action fests of the time (I imagine the VHS snuggled next to *Death Warrant*'s film siblings, like *Cobra* and *No Retreat, No Surrender*, like an action flick sandwich). Written by David S. Goyer (yes, film nerds, the guy who wrote *The Dark Knight* and other more recent superhero flicks, THAT David S. Goyer), it changes it up the standard formula a bit. We start the film where police officer Louis Burke (Van Damme) confronts serial killer The Sandman, who we find out killed Burke's partner. JCVD shoots the killer in the climax of the opening scene. We then find out that the police force, along with local politicians, make a special undercover sting operation inside a prison where inmates are beginning to die mysteriously. Van Damme agrees to go undercover as an inmate. Now the fun really starts. It becomes *Brubaker* on testosterone. On the inside he befriends TV's *Benson*, Robert Guillaume playing Hawkins, who actually did a nice job acting against type as a prisoner with a heart of gold. Of course, what action film would be complete without a love interest? This was no different as Cynthia Gibb's Amanda Beckett serves as his romantic liaison. She takes on the role as his fake undercover wife so she can give Burke what he needs to survive in prison, as well as info on the case… and then, of course, they fall for each other and get busy on a supposedly 'fake' conjugal visit (guess they were super deep undercover(s)). After surviving the usual prison fights and attempts to kill him, Burke discovers the nature of the deaths of the prisoners: they were murdered for their organs to be sold on the black market! Oh, true believer, it gets better: The Sandman was not dead! He was transferred to the same prison as Burke, and you can imagine the zaniness that ensues. I did learn something about inside the big house, though, the prison guards and prison doctors are vile villains and much worse than the inmates.

The finale was fun. A prison riot started by good ol' Sandman leads into the final showdown between our hero and The Sandman. One thing about *Death Warrant*, and pretty much all of JCVD's movies, are the karate spin kicks. I mean a shit ton. The same spin kick, over and over again. And it's like he goes into slow mo and the people getting the kick just stand there, watching him spin like a ballet dancer. It's like they're mesmerized. I can also say out of all the martial arts stars in movies Jean-Claude is far more fluid in his movements, and like I alluded to above, very smooth and graceful, like a dancer that can smash your teeth in.

I guess, thinking back, JCVD was an alternative to the other action heroes of his time. No, he didn't get any action figures, wasn't super huge and muscle-y, and even though he had an accent he sure wasn't Latino like me (come to think of it there wasn't any Latino action stars growing up, or any in this day and age, really… some things never change, I guess), but every time his movies were (are?) on TV I would watch. I must confess, I dislike most action flicks now (call me an old, snooty, film dork), but do love horror, Godzilla cheesefests, and yes, every now and then my inner twelve-year-old will sit and watch a ham-fisted shoot-em up, karate movie. Still, a Van Damme Special is no exception. And you know what? His acting was not bad. His charisma and those Euro good looks that made the ladies swoon in his prime didn't hurt either. If I was making a serious film and had the means I'd consider casting him against type as a heavy, no karate whatsoever, and let him go nuts. Imagine seeing Van Damme accepting an Oscar for portraying an overweight, bearded slum lord, Stallone-style a la *Cop Land*. If only.

So, if you have the hankerin' for some kicks, bang-bang shoot-em ups, and wanna watch a fun, fast (it clocked in just under 90 minutes), and pretty entertaining action yarn, then *Death Warrant* is not a bad choice. I mean, I've seen worse.

- Erick Gutierrez

Double Impact (1991)

I think if ever there was an actor inside JCVD, then *Double Impact* is the movie where he takes center stage. Alex and Chad Wagner are such great poles of the JCVD repertoire; one a perfumed L.A. prince, the other a Hong Kong hardened mercenary.

JCVD pulls both off in glorious splendor, so much so, the film is really polarizing, especially when they're on screen together. Of course, you all know the trick, but really this film illustrates how a one-time, one-act pony like JCVD can really shine opposite a co-star of equally size and ego. In this case...himself.

Sheldon Lettich followed JCVD on his rise to stardom, first as the writer of *Bloodsport*, then writing and directing for the Muscles from Brussels on *Lionheart* (aka *Wrong Bet*) as well as this movie. They would go on to other films, until Van Damme slowly became Van Done, but *Double Impact* is this dude in the audience's cream atop the crap.

The story is about as deep as a pygmy's wading pool; Chad and Alex are the sons of successful entrepreneur Paul Wagner. That won't help Paul out now though. See, after opening the Victoria Harbour tunnel, Paul and his wife are shot and killed by Bolo (yes Chong Li returns) aka Moon, while the baby JCVD twins are smuggled to safety by a maid and family friend Frank Avery (Geoffrey Lewis, *Tango & Cash*).

CUT TO.

SUPER: "25 YEARS LATER"

In sunny California Chad and Frank are operating a successful school where Chad gets to help hot chicks stretch out, all the while fantasizing about themselves with Chad partaking in some good, old-fashioned Californication. But flirting time is cut short when Frank tells Chad that he has something that could make them a little dough in the Far East.

Boom! We're back in Hong Kong, and soon Frank and Chad cross paths with Danielle Wilde (Alonna Shaw, *King of New York*). And what a wild girl she is. She has JCVD begging her to "keep going," as she slides her hands under his shorts and then bellow his black silk underwear till...

POW!

That's right sports fans. Alex shows up and gives his brother a good kick in the ass for coming on to *his* girlfriend. Frank then proceeds to try and convince Alex that Chad is indeed his twin brother (which maybe to them is a stretch, but to us, it's FUCKING OBVIOUS!). He also drops the revenge plot bombshell. See Mama and Popa Wagner were knocked off by their dodgy associate Griffith (Alan Scarfe, *Iron Eagle II*) and his mate Raymond Zhang (Philip Chan, following up from *Bloodsport*). Chad and Alex don't see eye to eye, and after a smuggling racket goes awry, Chad is mistaken for Alex, meets one his folk's murderers in the form of Zhang and, it turns out, Danielle has been working for Griffith. She begins to dig on Alex's insistence to find out if the t-shirt old Frank is trying to sell him is on the level, as far as his parents and the tunnel and so forth.

The rest of the movie from here is Chad and Alex learning to get along so they can go along; get some righteous payback for Mom and Dad. Danielle begins to pick up the paper trail, but she is being watched, closely and seductively, by Ms. Olympia Cory Everson's Kara. It even gets a little kinky between the girls so...enjoy.

The boys move to deserted resort to prepare to take on their enemies by pretending to bring Zhang cases of the finest Cognac, but they're really bombs. But Chad fucks up and Alex reminds him. Needless to say, the fuck up costs the boys Zhang (he gets away), and Danielle (after that kinky scene I just mentioned) calls the resort/hideout and tells Chad she was searched by a 'security person'. Because Frank and Alex are out doing man-stuff, Chad steals the boat and heads off to pick up Danielle. Alex gets drunk and starts imagining his brother and his girl doing the horizontal folk dance on voyage back to the hideout.

Chad gets back with Danielle in time to have his lights put out by Alex. The brothers say balls to the whole deal and agree not to darken each other's doors again. Danielle's call to the resort was however, intercepted by Griffith who sends out the triads. Frank and Danielle are taken hostage after the scrap is officially over, and the JCVD boys beat it out of one of the surviving triads as to the location of their friends and enemies.

Thus, we all assemble for fight night on Zhang's pier of destiny. All the good guys and the bad guys make an appearance. Chad has a couple of the cooler moments. He gets to take on Chong li/Moon/Bolo one more time, and he gets to kill Griffith by dropping a bloody shipping container on his head. In a word...priceless!

So, the brother's Wagner at last achieve their long-awaited hour of retribution. They might have very well returned for a sequel if JCVD and Lettich were able to better wrangle the rights away from the various entities controlling film. Van Damme spoke once of his vision of a sequel with a far more serious tone. I for one can't see it, and I can safely say there'll be a remake before there's a sequel. Still, I am grateful for the guys that made *Bloodsport*. That team came up nicely through the years, ultimately leaving us with their legacy, alongside the movie that Van Damme thought would show folks out there...he was in fact...a two-trick pony.

- Kent Hill

Universal Soldier (1992)

I remember liking *Universal Soldier* when I first saw it on cable back in 1992 or '93. Good hook, with dead veterans resurrected by the U.S. government to work as emotionless commandos; good directing and story from Roland Emmerich, who would go on to make loads of huge tentpole movies like *Independence Day* and *2012*; and decent acting from stars Jean-Claude Van Damme and Dolph Lundgren.

And I think that was the real hook behind the movie when it was announced: The two had made a lot of memorable action flicks on their own. But seeing two action heroes like JCVD and Lundgren – maybe lesser-known icons than Stallone or Schwarzenegger, but still stars – getting together and kicking ass was a first. Remember, this was decades before the *Expendables* series made it far more common.

I was expecting it to be pretty rough (I hadn't seen it in years), but you know what? The movie still holds up. It doesn't feel dated at all. The tech, costumes, and everything else are just general enough to make it feel like it could've been made far more recently than 28 years ago. The only thing that really makes it feel older is its characters' reliance on landlines to make phone calls. If anything, with the lack of trust of Americans for their government these days, the story it tells may be even more timely today.

The fact is the movie is eminently watchable. It's entertaining. The action is nonstop. Not a moment of screen time is wasted. The moments of humor sprinkled through the script are well-paced – mostly involving the zombie-like JCVD dealing with normal people. "Universal Soldier" is obviously science fiction, but seeing it again made me realize it's as much horror as it is SF.

But I have a theory: I think this movie was secretly subversive.

Looking back at it with a critical eye after nearly 30 years, I was struck by just how revolutionary the movie is. Tackling the idea of soldiers killed in unnecessary wars later being revived as the living dead to fight for their country again is crazy. Especially for a movie made almost immediately in the wake of Operation: Desert Storm, and most especially for what is – on the surface – merely a high-profile action movie. It makes me think the people involved weren't paying too much attention to the movie's subtext (such as it is). Fans certainly didn't. They no doubt only saw what I saw back in the day: An action movie with musclebound martial artists kicking the crap out of each other.

There's also the steroid angle. A couple of already buff and tough fighting dudes get even buffer and tougher by injecting themselves with a miracle drug that makes them invincible. Stallone was making boxing movies with training montages and Schwarzenegger was playing cyborgs, but would either of them have made a movie about their muscles getting chemical enhancement? Being less-famous stars has its merits.

Deeper than usual material for a simple action movie, right? I mean, it's not high art or sophisticated commentary or anything, but *Universal Soldier* obviously has a lot more going on below the surface than either the makers acknowledged during filming, or executives and fans realized upon viewing.

I haven't intentionally seen any of the sequels. I vaguely remember happening to catch *Universal Soldier: The Return* on cable at some point and managing to sit through it. Nothing really memorable about it. Then there were a bunch of direct-to-video sequels, whose titles I'm not going to bother looking up. Those looked pretty terrible, especially as cash-grabs for a movie that wasn't an enormous to begin with.

If you haven't watched *Universal Soldier* since it came out (or it's been a shorter while), revisit it. You might get a newfound appreciation for it.

- Kurt Belcher

Nowhere to Run (1993)

In many people's minds, including my own, the most entertaining actor among the group of the elite action stars of the 80's and 90's was Jean-Claude Van Damme. From his wild barroom dance scene in *Bloodsport* to his painful looking splits all over the dang place. (See *Timecop.*) On rare occasions, he prefers filling his time co-starring in the new ongoing film series "The Expendables" alongside most of the remaining 80's and 90's action superstars.

Jean-Claude was born Jean-Claude Camille François Van Varenberg in Brussels in the municipality of Sint-Agatha-Berchem in 1960 on the 18th of October.

Nowhere To Run is set in the countryside, which added a new feel to his usual plots. It never gets old watching Van Damme knuckle up and fight his way through country thugs with precision just to defend an innocent family from being forced from their home and property. Time after time, he saves the day, all without a single strand of hair being out of place. For me it will always be a classic 90's action free-for-all.

Even before I had time to fully appreciate the amazing prison transport escape trope, I was impressed with the cinematography, delivered by David Gribble, who was also the director of photography for the film. The sharp desert skylines beam endless lens flare as the newly emancipated Van Damme, who plays Sam Gillen, tries to maintain his freedom.

Sam's young accomplice, Billy, played by Anthony Starke, shows up in his hotrod and gets the prison bus to shimmy, shimmy, flip over onto the driver's side. Sam escapes via the "broken leg" bit he feeds to the corrections officer with the keys and runs to the stylish muscle car where his partner was waiting. Sam and Billy toss the other escapees out of the vehicle and began racing down the dusty highway.

Another trope I would like to point out is the buddy-escapee relationship, which lasted about 8 minutes until Sam watches Billy die after being shot by another freed passenger during their last Hail Mary spree. I guess they didn't like getting thrown out of the car.

For my money, the second scene, which takes place in a quick shop, was as spot on as a 90's action flick interaction could ever aspire to be. Let me quote it for you:

– **Country Store Clerk:** What you doin' out this way?

– **Sam Gillen:** Hunting.

– **Country Store Clerk:** In a suit? What kinda huntin'?

– **Sam Gillen:** Pink flamingos.

Pink fucking flamingos, and what may very well have been the movies best mic drops.

Overall, the first act was a lot of fun. Sam was only looking to hideout in the vast countryside until things died down enough to make his final dash to freedom. This plan is threatened as he comes across a small family being harassed by ruthless but not very smart land developers trying to force them to leave their property. Sam, as with similar tales, now has a tough decision to make. On one hand, he has freedom nipping at his tail, and on the other, a family who desperately needs his specific brand of help. So, should he save himself from the local police, or should he risk it all - his escape, his plans, his freedom - all to save a small family he never met before.

At the beginning of the second act, you immediately see which path our lone wolf protector chose. After all, most newly escaped convicts love stalling out their plan to freedom and taking a chance at losing it all again for people he doesn't even remotely know. He's a better man than I am; I'd be out of that piece in a hot second. Don't judge.

Van Damme gave a rather stale performance of the generic character we all know and root for. This is a typical recycled full-on action-palooza.

Just remember, amazing acting and award worthy performances are not why you watch a Jean-Claude Van Damme film. You watch these types of action movies as an escape. Hopefully, you'll get to experience some sweet, over-the-top action, a few solid one-liners, and possibly a decent story. This epic blockbuster absolutely delivers all of it repeatedly.

Rosanna Arquette playing this particular damsel in distress, Clydie, was less than believable or convincing. She is a fantastic actor in so many other films that I absolutely adore. It was quite cringy when she tried delivering some of the emotional elements of her character. She nailed her role as the strong-willed, hardheaded widow and mother of two, so she did pull off the performance better than the film required.

A young Kieran Culkin – yes, *that* Culkin – gave an award-winning performance as Mike. He always blows my mind. His work was excellent, and through all the over-the-top action sequences, subplots, and textbook love scenes, his performance was one of the best bits of work throughout the entire movie. His character was captivating as he played the role of the often-used fatherless boy. I have read that he and Van Damme instantly had great chemistry in every scene they were in together.

I gave it a go and read the whole poorly written script; that's another four hours of my life I'll never get back. The writers did not seem like they were too fond of using subplots. They tried to keep it simple, single-minded, and focused, and voila!!

It turned out that it wasn't a piece of dung, as many action flicks of the day seemed to be. For the thralls of Jean-Claude Van Damme fans, I'm sure most of you have already seen it. If not, you should fix that by going to watch it immediately, and afterwards, please take the time to rethink your life decisions.

No, there will not be any chatter about the ending, as not to spoil it for those who have yet to indulge in this crumb of cinematic excellence.

- Stan Konopka

Last Action Hero (1993)

Writing about *Last Action Hero* is a fun diversion from the other contents of this book because of one thing: Cameos. There are a shit ton of cameos in the flick, including a blink-and-you'll-miss-him cameo from JCVD at the end, attending the premiere of Schwarzenegger's latest (fictional) action opus, "Jack Slater IV".

Now that we've got that out of the way, we can talk about the movie itself, which is far more interesting than it deserves to be. Despite the fact that *Last Action Hero* was a notorious box office bomb, it was very much ahead of its time. The movie is metafictional in the extreme, before meta was a common term that everyone and their brother knew about. I love that so many fictional worlds seem to be contained within this one, like Whiskers the cartoon cat (voiced by Danny DeVito). Also, "real" fictional worlds are in there, including F. Murray Abraham as Slater's former police ally, John Practice. However, in a running joke, Abraham (the actor) is recognized by Danny Madigan, Jack Slater's kid sidekick from the real world, as Salieri, who 'killed' Mozart in Miloš Forman's *Amadeus*. He keeps warning Slater that Practice is going to betray him. There's also a black-and-white detective (like literally B&W in a color scene) played by a Bogart lookalike.

Of course, telling meta stories is something that plenty of comics (*The Unwritten*), books (*House of Leaves*), movies (*Stranger Than Fiction*), cartoons (*Family Guy*), and TV shows (*Fleabag*) have since visited more times that I can remember. But in 1993, this was a fairly new idea for the average moviegoer.

1993 was also a banner year for Schwarzenegger. He was at the height of his fame, having just come off of the biggest hit of his career up to that point, *Terminator 2: Judgment Day*. At this point a starring vehicle for Schwarzenegger was essentially a guarantee of butts in seats, and a license to print money. Hollywood producers and fans felt like he could do no wrong. So, it came as a huge shock when the movie hit and underperformed. Compared to *T2*, which cost at least $94–102 million and grossed $520.9 million, *Last Action Hero* cost $85 million and only made $137.3 million at the box office. He went from his biggest to his biggest flop in two movies.

The director, John McTiernan, was at the top of his game at the same time. McTiernan was responsible for making some of the biggest action movies of a decade, from 1987's *Predator* (another – far more popular – Schwarzenegger vehicle), 1988's *Die Hard* (which helped make Bruce Willis an action star), and 1990's *The Hunt for Red October.*

Then there's writer Shane Black. With McTiernan and Schwarzenegger, Black made a name helping to invent the modern action movie by writing the first movie in the *Lethal Weapon* series. (I thought I remembered hearing that Black sold the script for some astronomical price. After checking that fact, I realized I'd mixed it up with 1991's *The Last Boy Scout*, a similarly titled – and similarly underperforming – action flick Black had also written.)

Let's face it: Any one of these elements should've added up to the biggest blockbuster action movie of 1993. All of them together should've added up to one of the biggest movies of all time. So, what went wrong? I can't really say. I'm not a movie critic, after all. I'm just playing one in this essay. Still, I see a few possibilities.

It's honestly a very weird flick that goes in a lot of different directions. It's stuffed with satire, and switches gears from action to comedy and back again at the drop of a hat. Also, the shift in tone halfway through the movie, when fictional character "Jack Slater" jumps into the real world, is masterfully done. Going from the bright, stylized world of film to dark, dreary real life works beautifully.

That may also be the movie's problem. It likely threw off audiences who were looking for a simple Schwarzenegger popcorn flick. But when an action hero learns that he's just a character being played by "the famous comedian Arnold Braunschweiger", it gets very dark. The real world's not perfect like the perpetual California of the movies. Things don't always come out right in the end. The action hero doesn't always save the day. He's not perfect, not indestructible, doesn't necessarily catch the bad guy.

Pretty deep stuff for a simple summer movie.

Still, "LAH" doesn't forget to be a satire. It takes jabs at so many action movies tropes and clichés, it makes your head spin. In addition to JCVD, there are cameos from Sharon Stone as Catherine Tramell from *Basic Instinct* and Robert Patrick as the T-1000 from *T2*. The movie doesn't quite make all these clichés work again, but it does get a lot of ironic mileage out of them. McTiernan even parodies the Hans Gruber death scene from his own movie, *Die Hard*, when we see Jack Slater falling off a building in a nearly identical shot.

Also, I'd actually watch some of those fake "Jack Slater" movies, especially the one with the criminally underrated Tom Noonan playing the Ripper (as well as playing himself).

Of course, speaking of villains, the true draw there is Charles Dance. Modern fans will know Dance as the wicked family patriarch, Tywin Lannister, from HBO's *Game of Thrones*. However, he first played a deliciously villainous role in Eddie Murphy's *The Golden Child*. He doesn't disappoint as Benedict, the highly intelligent but subservient villain to Anthony Quinn's Vivaldi, the main villain of "Jack Slater IV" (one of many movies-within-the-movie). By interfering with the world of the movie, Danny makes Benedict realize he's actually in a movie and he can get out of said movie. When he crosses over into the real world, he becomes far more dangerous than any action movie villain could be.

If you haven't seen *Last Action Hero*, check it out. Thankfully, JCVD is barely in it.

- Kurt Belcher

Hard Target (1993)

Hard Target was the first Hollywood film directed by famed Hong Kong action director, John Woo, who fled his home country before it reunified with mainland China in 1997. Woo brought some of his operatic vision and dynamic style with him. But sadly, not his clarity of vision, nor his powerful character arcs. Woo delivered an, at times, exciting, slick actioner. But it is also uneven. It is laughably over the top at times, and ultimately unsatisfying.

The story is an implausible modern variation of *The Most Dangerous Game.* It is more over-the-top than operatic, devoid as it is of cohesive themes and meaningful character arcs – two things that always marked Woo's best work.

Hollywood prefers formulas over originality. Even Sam Raimi (his Renaissance Pictures produced), a stylish director himself, seemed content to rein the master in, and indulged him only token snatches of stylish finesse.

The movie, set in recession-torn New Orleans, opens with homeless vet Doug Binder (scripter Chuck Pfarrer) being chased by a well-oiled mob of mercenaries. The group is led by Fouchon (Lance Henriksen), the elitist mastermind, and Van Cleaf (Arnold Vosloo, of *Darkman* sequels), the muscle. Binder is taken down with a steel arrow shot from an air rifle by their wealthy "client."

Nat (short for Natasha) Binder (Yancy Brown), Doug's daughter, comes to town searching for her dad. At a café she flashes a wad of cash when paying for her coffee. Three punks follow her out and try to hold her up. But also in the diner is Chance Boudreaux (JCVD), a homeless Cajun, who observes the punks, follows them out, and knocks them senseless.

He is the moral heart of the film, but a canned, static one. Nat hires Chance to help her in her quest.

First stop is a mission. Here Woo takes pains to include evocative shots of the homeless in the impoverished city. It makes for a moving backdrop to otherwise routine plot exposition. They meet Elisha Roper (Willie Carpenter), a homeless friend. He leads them to Doug's discarded shopping cart. There they find pornographic leaflets he was passing out for money.

This leads them to morally bankrupt Randal Poe (Eliott Keener), who distributes the leaflets. They press him for info, but are interrupted when Van Cleaf comes in. Chance meets his steely glare, and each know the other is a formidable opponent.

The police discover Doug's body, burned in a warehouse fire. The body has only one dog tag. Chance, knowing they come in twos, goes back to comb the ashes at the burn site. He finds the tag, with a hole in it from a tri-barbed arrowhead.

But the next hunt is already underway. Randal hires Elisha for the next target. Fouchon and Van Cleaf explain the rules of the hunt to a new client. They find only ex-military, who give them a more-sporting hunt. They selected New Orleans for its unrest. They have conducted hunts in all kinds of desperate places throughout the world.

Elisha is given a money belt with 10 grand inside it. If he can get to the river, he is told, it is his. Elisha makes a run, but the team surrounds him in cemetery. He manages to take the client's gun and kill him. Elisha runs into the streets of New Orleans and begs Ted Raimi for help. Ted chews up the scenery with his usual aplomb, telling Elisha he doesn't have any change. Finally, Elisha is gunned down in a busy street by a veritable motorcade, in very unlikely fashion.

Chance and Nat are attacked by mercenaries. Chance and Nat flee on stolen a motorcycle, chased by bad guys. Here the action goes laughably over-the-top as Chance stands on the moving motorcycle, shooting two fisted.

They escape to his Uncle Douvee's wilderness Cajun hold up. Douvee is a marvelous turn by Wilford Brimley. He gives Chance a pump shotgun, and Chance goes off alone on horseback to hunt the bad guys.

Douvee's place is invaded by the mercenaries. He shoots an arrow and sets off a booby trapped still, blowing up a bunch of baddies. Brimley has a great hero shot at the end of this sequence on horseback, holding his bow triumphantly aloft, with a big explosion backing him.

Chance is tracked to an abandoned factory that houses Mardi Gras floats. And here the movie finds some badly needed pep. Shades of *Southern Comfort,* Cajun Chance moves stealthily through the warehouse, picking off mercenaries in ingenious ways. The action is stylish and well-mounted, and the colorful floats make a provocative backdrop. There have been many shots of doves throughout the film, and here the motif comes to fruition. The place is full of them, and they shit on mercenaries, helping Chance in his battle on more than one occasion. At one point a bird lands on his shoulder and he gently coos to it like they are old pals. Douvee's name is also likely a patois variation of the word "dove." It's a colorful flourish that echoes back to Woos previous HK films. He draws a contrast between the "natural" Cajuns and those trapped by social constructs. But it doesn't add up to much else.

Chance takes out Van Cleaf in a scene very reminiscent of *Hard Boiled,* in which they run on opposite sides of a windowed wall, firing at one another through the glass. Chance takes a grenade from Van Cleaf and drops it down Fouchon's pants.

Fouchon manages to retrieve the grenade and defuse it. Henriksen has a short-lived moment of triumph, until a stray spark ignites the device. "Whoops," he says, and is blown to bits. It is a tour-de-force moment for Henriksen.

For all its shortcomings, *Hard Target* still remains my favorite JCVD movie, and it's not a bad way to spend 96 minutes. Watered down Woo is still better than 99 percent of programmers. However, all the characters are cardboard, start to finish, and therein lies *Hard Target*'s greatest failing.

- Ron Ford

Time Cop (1994)

The black rain continued to fall as he scuttled through the junkyard, rusted shards of jagged metal determining his path through the debris.

He didn't even really want to be there. He much preferred to stay off the roads, but the interminable pang of an empty stomach drew him to the yard. The last time he'd eaten meat was in a junkyard, where he'd come across a den of mice. So overcome at the sight, he grabbed the litter in two handfuls and ate them with not more than two bites.

However, that was two years ago (or was it three?) and the chances that any rodents were still left anywhere on this God-forsaken plant was practically nil. But one had to try and he could almost taste the meat just thinking about it.

The rain intensified; the acid-tinged ash burned as it dispersed on his skin. He needed to get under shelter. Then he saw the minivan. A 1998 Dodge Caravan. He knew it on sight. A flash of memory stole across his mind. Getting picked up after soccer practice. Going through the McDonalds drive-thru, the French fry grease stubbornly refusing to stain his polyester jersey.

While that world was gone, the Caravan was in the here and now. He pulled at the sliding door handle half expecting it to come off in his hands.

But it opened. And he jumped inside the dry interior. They were piles of garbage and old clothing and the fetid stench of deterioration. But it was dry. He closed the door, took off his hat and began to loosen his coat when he saw it.

There under one of the piles of clothing was a familiar green font, ironically spelling out the very thing he was inside at the moment. Another artifact of a world that no longer existed.

"God damn," he thought. Van Damme. *Time Cop*.

Like a sign from the bearded magical man in the sky, there it was. His all-time favorite fucking movie. It had been at least twenty years since he'd even seen a movie. The thought of actually spending ninety minutes doing something other than sleeping, grubbing for food or just trying to stay alive seemed like something that never existed, yet he knew that it had.

And for a flash, he suddenly wished that he could waste ninety minutes of his life enjoying the greatest fucking movie of all time. But he knew that was not in the cards.

And just then he saw it. The faint glow of electricity. A green light. It might as well have been a supernova, but there it was staring him right in the face.

This fucking van has power.

He didn't ask how. And frankly, he didn't care. His pulse quickened. He looked up instinctively to the center console on the back bench of the minivan and there it was. A DVD screen. Was he dreaming? Was he dead? No. This was real, this was happening.

Slowly he reached for the DVD, knowing that his dream could only come true if the silver disc was actually inside. He could hardly breathe. He opened the case; the snapping plastic latches caught him off guard. It was a sound he instantly knew yet had forgotten a million years ago.

But there it was, in all of its glory. *Time Cop*. The DVD was ready and so was he. He pulled it out from the case, and out of a habit burned into muscle memory eons ago he scanned the backside for scratches. If Powerball still existed, this was the day to get a ticket. It was clean. Perfectly clean.

He began to cry.

With tears forging paths through the dirt in his face, he slipped the disc into the player and held his breath. The glow of the title credits flickered on to the screen.

The sound of the pouring rain hitting the van roof almost perfectly matched the rain in the opening scene, as Confederate soldiers confront the mysterious stranger, who aims his out-of-time laser site on them and blows them all away with his machine pistols before stealing their gold.

And then just like that it was the future. Well, their future. 1994 was ancient history as far as he was concerned. But he quashed that thought immediately and dived back into an escape from reality that was better than heroin.

So, he watched as the story unfolded.

The Time Enforcement Commission (TEC) needs to clean up the timeline, with Confederate gold paying for terrorist weapons.

'Time for a hero to step up,' he thought as he for a split-second thought he smelled popcorn.

As he watched, he couldn't help but wonder why he loved this movie. But really, he knew why.

Jean Claude Van Damme,

In an era of squinty-eye faux martial arts douches like Steven Seagal, Van Damme made his character, DC Metro Police officer Max Walker, seem downright likable. Not aloof. Not a cauldron of simmering anger waiting to barrel kick someone through a plate-glass window. Just a guy with a hot wife (who is killed in a house explosion) trying to do his job.

And that's what made this movie work. The plot was fine. Good guys, bad guys. The script was decent. No Oscars were in the offing, but no roll-your-eyes dialogue either.

Decent special effects and good directing kept the story moving as Walker takes on a corrupt Senator and a turncoat partner before realizing he can use the time machine to save his wife and kill the bad guy.

And as he sat in the 1998 Dodge Caravan watching the story unfold, he realized why this movie spoke to him, especially now.

Walker's life was ruined, but he found a way to help himself fix it. It was a message. It had to be. A minivan with power? How? He never even bothered to check. He really didn't want to know.

A minivan with power with a working DVD player? With a pristine copy of his favorite movie? What were the odds?

It had to be a message. "I can fix this," he thought.

He just needed a time machine.

But first, he needed to eat.

Now where was that mouse?

- Jon Arking

"Time Won't Let Me" (1994)

The Smithereens and Jean-Claude Van Damme. Honestly, it's a perfect pairing. Like a fine bottle of Beaujolais with roast duck, or more appropriately to this scenario, a Belgian beer with roasted Jersey raccoon. Their collaboration on "Time Won't Let Me" for 1994's *Timecop* resulted in what may have been the mainstream peak for both. For the Smithereens, the ultimate New Jersey garage band (sorry Bon Jovi, but you'll find very little hair spray in their backstage) covering The Outsider's 1966 hit made perfect sense. The Outsiders, from Cleveland, were also considered a working-class garage band. "Time Won't Let Me" (which was their first release) was also their only Top 10, going to Number 5. And while the Smithereens' highest comparable charting hit was 1991's "Too Much Passion," which peaked at Number 37, having their cover become *Timecop*'s anthem and including Van Damme in the accompanying video, exposed them to a mass audience they might never have otherwise reached. While Van Damme already had a tried-and-true following, *Timecop* was his highest grossing film ($100 million) and also put him in front of millions of people who might have only watched *Universal Soldier* or *Lionheart* on video.

But putting all of that aside, what makes this video work is that it is fun to watch. It would have been very easy to simply edit together a bunch of clips from the movie and roll them over the top of the song and call it a day. And frankly, if it had been a Steven Seagal or Chuck Norris movie, that's probably what they would have done. What makes this video different is they put Van Damme in it, as himself. In fact, he leads of the video telling the band that he will lead them through time, to which they giving a, "Sure, whatever" nod. Van Damme then looks into the camera and says, "Let's do it" at which point the band kicks into the opening riff of "Time Won't Let Me." Yes, there are clips of the movie (of course with splits aplenty) interspersed throughout. After all it is Hollywood.

But the movie clips are at about a 50-50 ratio to video clips of the band and Van Damme goofing around including a quick stint on what at first appears to be an air harmonica, but on closer examination is an actual harmonica, no doubt borrowed from Bruce Willis. In addition, the clips that are interspersed through the video, are synced up with the clips of the band. So, when clips from 1929 are shown, out come the fedoras. The Civil War-era scenes are followed by the band in Confederate uniforms, somewhat confused and bemused at their sudden change in wardrobe, while rain pours down on the band as clips of the same are shown. All throughout, Van Damme is pushing buttons and moving levers on the (straight out of the Sci-Fi Props Department) set, which is simultaneously a time machine (?) and recording studio.

The key is Van Damme's ability to (and please take note Chuck and Steve) FUCKING MAKE FUN OF HIMSELF. Van Damme seems to understand that when they director yells "Cut!" it's time to put the ego down along with the script. I mean, honestly, just look at 2016's Jean-Claude Van Johnson. Can you imagine Norris or Seagal starring in a series making fun of their own abilities? Mocking the very nature of their stardom? Nope, me neither. (Although there are times you'd like to think some of the crap they've put out was actually a giant spoof, but alas no)

I would argue that the same could be said for the Smithereens. They were a band that had ambition and obvious talent (catchy hooks with simple, but interesting word play) but never seemed to take themselves too seriously. I experienced that firsthand when I interviewed the band's lead singer Pat DiNizio in 1992. I was a HUGE fan after 1988's *Green Thoughts* (with iconic Alt Rock hits like "Only a Memory" and "House We Used to Live In") and found him to be a total professional, yet fun. I'm sure I was the 47th interview he'd done that day with doofus DJ's like myself asking the same doofus questions, but you would never have known. He was engaging and a thoroughly likable guy. And while I never had a chance to interview Van Damme, I'd like to believe he'd be the same way. I'm not basing that off anything more than my hunch that anyone who can make fun of themselves is unlikely to be a total douchebag.

So where does that leave us? At this point, at about 800 words, which is 200 less than I promised. Hey, let's see you churn out one thousand words on a fucking four-minute video! Let me say that again; let's see you churn out one thousand words (that's one more than nine hundred and ninety-nine and one less than one thousand and one if you're wondering) on a four-minute video. Seriously that is a lot of words. About a nearly 30-year-old video of a nearly 30-year-old movie. I could comment on the blonde perm that Van Damme is rocking in the video, which as far as a I can tell was not in the movie *Timecop*. I could, but what would be the point? Obviously, the video was shot at some point after the movie and Van Damme had moved on to other projects. I suppose I could check and see. Hang on...

Yep. *Street Fighter*. Blonde perm. Okay. About fifty words left. I guess it wouldn't be a good idea to start talking about *Street Fighter*. That will be in the next chapter, and I don't want to be rude. So, I will stick with The Smithereens' "Time Won't Let Me" from the 1994 movie *Timecop* which stars Jean-Claude Van Damme and that is a thousand words, making me a man of my word, if not creativity.

- Jon Arking

Street Fighter (1994)

To paraphrase that great bard William Shakespeare, "I come here not to bury *Street Fighter*, but to praise it."

Released to withering reviews in 1994, the Jean-Claude Van Damme-led adaptation of Capcom's ultra-popular fighting game franchise has long been a pop-cultural whipping boy on par with Vanilla Ice and Rob Schneider. Like many films from an earlier era, though, it's important to look at *Street Fighter* in the context of its time.

In the early '90s, video games were not yet taken seriously as a form of art. They were toys meant for children, nothing more. As even the *Mortal Kombat* movie would find with its release one year later, critics were loath to acknowledge a video game adaptation's redeeming qualities, even when they turned out rather good.

Street Fighter wasn't nearly as good that first *Mortal Kombat* movie, but the creative decisions writer-director Steven de Souza made don't look so bad when you consider his position not as an arcade-dwelling die-hard, but as an outsider trying to translate the appeal of a relatively young and still very crude medium to a wider audience.

The biggest deviation from the source material that gamers tend to cite as a "flaw" in *Street Fighter* was its plot. Remember that it's based on a fighting game, though, a genre not known for having particularly strong or original narratives. It's also Japanese, which means it sometimes gets very… odd.

For those of you who don't know the plot of the classic Street Fighter games (i.e. most people) here's the Cliff's Notes:

The first game is about a pair of martial artists, Ryu and Ken, entering a fighting tournament. That's it. The second game, which made the franchise famous, rehashes the tournament angle but this time it's used as ploy so M. Bison, leader of a crime organization called Shadaloo, can lure the world's greatest fighters into one place and brainwash them to help him take over the world.

Some of the characters have connections to one another. Many don't. Some of the characters also have supernatural powers, which are largely unexplained (or explained goofily, such as Blanka being green because he's a vegetarian and having electricity powers because he got hit by lightning once).

Imagine being a first-time American filmmaker asked to turn this nonsensical, wafer-thin story full of weird, wildly dissimilar characters into a mainstream action blockbuster. Did I mention that Street Fighter was only the second video game-adapted movie ever made? Or that the first one was the even less well-remembered *Super Mario Bros.*? Or that the treatment was drafted in one night so Universal Pictures could secure the rights?

To his credit, de Souza has said he wanted to avoid trotting out the tournament gimmick again. Instead, he chose the far ballsier option of trying to tell an actual story. And, shockingly, with a roster of 16 fan-favorite characters to sift through, de Souza somehow managed to find enough screen time for all but one (a Bruce Lee clone named Fei Long).

It wasn't easy. Changes had to be made. Backstories had to be tweaked (sometimes a little, sometimes a lot) to ensure that all the characters had substantive reasons to interact with one another. Magical fighting moves had to be toned down (Ryu's Hadoken no longer launched a fireball), rooted in real-world technology (M. Bison's flight was driven by electromagnetism rather than "Psycho Power"), or removed entirely (Dhalsim's Plastic Man-esque stretchy limbs became just… normal limbs).

In an attempt to make M. Bison's dictatorial aspirations believable, de Souza chose to emphasize the villain's paramilitary trappings, reimagining Shadaloo as a terroristic private army. With that in mind, who better to challenge M. Bison (played with mad-eyed brilliance by Raul Julia in his final role) than the franchise's other big military-themed character, Guile (Van Damme)?

Suddenly, all the characters having such disparate backgrounds made sense; if M. Bison was a worldwide threat, he could be opposed by a United Nations-backed counterterrorist operation, one whose troops would include British femme-fatale Cammy (played by pop-star Kylie Minogue, who Van Damme admitted to having a cocaine-fueled on-set affair with) and Indigenous Mexican bruiser T. Hawk.

Additionally, M. Bison being a terrorist provided an avenue for interesting plot complications, such as Chun Li's quest for vengeance now being pursued under the guise of a war correspondent news reporter. How the hell could de Souza justify Balrog, a boxer, and E. Honda, a sumo wrestler, getting involved in an international terrorist conflict? By having M. Bison's criminal allies ruin their athletic careers through fixing, prompting them to help Chun Li as payback!

Naturally, gamers weren't too pleased with these alterations. Ryu and Ken as roguish con men? Dhalsim as a scientist? Blanka as a mutated super-soldier? Nevertheless, such changes look a lot more practical when viewed from de Souza's perspective.

There were three ways *Street Fighter* could've gone:

1. De Souza could've told a fairly coherent story while making a few changes to series lore.
2. De Souza could've told a *more* coherent story by deleting many beloved characters entirely.
3. De Souza could've kept all the characters' lore intact, at the expense of *any* story coherence.

Considering de Souza's background as a screenwriter (his credits include *Die Hard*, *Commando*, and, uh, *The Flintstones*), it's not surprising he chose the first option. In fact, it's admirable he didn't go with the second one. And he didn't have pretentions about what he was creating either. De

Souza always knew he was making schlock, so he opted to have fun with it.

No surprise, then, that *Street Fighter*'s greatest strengths are its sense of humor and camp. The exasperated snark of Dee Jay and the lunatic narcissism of M. Bison are constant sources of amusement throughout, and if you don't die laughing when dumber-than-dirt Zangief responds to a TV live-feed showing a truck barreling towards him by screaming "QUICK! CHANGE THE CHANNEL!" then you have no soul.

Street Fighter is not a bad movie. Nor is it a good one. Rather, it's an endearing curio, an early stab at a then-new idea whose director contorted himself into pretzels attempting to please his audience.

At least he tried. If you want to see what happens when no one tries, sit through the entirety of 2009's colorless *Street Fighter: The Legend of Chun Li*.

I'll bet you a Bison Dollar you can't.

- William Tea

Street Fighter: The Movie (1995, video game)

What should you do when you make a movie based off a video game, but you also want to make more money off of the movie? You make a video game of the movie that was based off of a video game! *Street Fighter: The Movie: The Game* was Capcom's attempt to capitalize off the *Street Fighter* franchise while the movie was being shot. What would happen is that instead of the usual *Street Fighter* game made by Capcom, Capcom would hire a third party to shoot digitized images of the film's cast and use them in the game.

Capcom had hired Incredible Technologies to develop the game – which, at the time, would be the largest project for the small company to handle. The staff of the company would fly to the set of the movie being filmed and during that time, record shots of the actors striking poses and doing moves to be used in the game. This ultimately would all then be put together for the arcade and two at home consoles – the Sony PlayStation and the Sega Dreamcast.

While it should come as no surprise, the graphics in the arcade were miles better than the graphics on the at-home consoles. However, due to time constraints, certain characters were not released in the arcade version that the home versions got to experience. The arcade version is closer to the other games in the franchise with a tournament style of fighting. Once the character beats all of the others, a short story pops up and explains what the character did after defeating Bison.

The at-home versions of the game also have this mode along with other modes, including street battle, versus mode, and trial mode. The mode that will be focused on for the remaining of this review is the movie battle mode – which takes Guile through a series of opponents until he ultimately faces off against S. Bison. Yes, Super Bison.

Although the game did not receive a lot of praise, the fact that the console versions included this story mode is rather fun. This game was released in 1995 at a time where it was normal to see these tournament fighters play out with a small story line. Here, a single player can take Guile on a journey that almost feels out of a "choose your own adventure" book. Guile talks with Cammy throughout the entire story line but during these conversations, he can make the choice to go down different pathways. Picking certain pathways leads to a shorter road to face Bison while other choices can leave Guile fighting more characters. Once Guile makes it to the end, he has to face off against Bison twice – once as regular old Bison but after defeat, the player gets a short clip from the movie where Bison is injected with that cocktail mix that transforms him into Super Bison. After beating Super Bison, Guile's story ends in a similar still-photographed fashion as the movie.

Unfortunately, I did not have an opportunity to play this game. However, looking at old reviews, it's summed up as being "just okay." As a part of the *Street Fighter* franchise, some felt like this was the worst game out of the bunch. Others, while not huge fans, felt it was something different. While there were plenty of negative reviews, there were some positives that made it seem as if the game was enjoyable. For instance, there was a digitized image version of Akuma. While not in the film, he made his way into the video game, which had never been seen before.

As for the appearances by JCVD, it has been confirmed that he did record his digitized images and lent his voice to the game. This is the first time in video game history that a player can play as Jean-Claude Van Damme. Although the game may not have had great reviews, JC's portrayal of a digitized version of Guile looks great in the arcade version. But just like with any fighting video game, sometimes the grunts and one-liners get to be too much and can make even the biggest Van Damme fan start to cringe. There's only so much one can take when hearing the same sounds repeatedly while button mashing the controller.

My one wish is that the game followed suit to the other Street Fighter games in that they followed up on the defeated screen by making up the characters to look like they were beaten up and defeated. But in this case, all we get to see is Guile saying that the opponent should never mess with a man who has his own army while a still, gray photograph of the opponent looks off the screen like a rejected headshot. Overall, if a fan wants to play a game with Van Damme in it, or a super *Street Fighter* fan needed to complete their list, then this game is a must-play. For those that don't care as much but are still interested in the gameplay, do what I did and find a playthrough video of the arcade and console versions.

- John Bruske

Sudden Death (1995)

Ah, *Sudden Death.* I swear this movie is my childhood and teenage years put onto the silver screen. No. I was not a fire marshal hired to check out old Civic Arena in Pittsburgh for game seven of the Stanley Cup Playoffs. However, I was a gigantic hockey nut in the 90s, and still am to some degree today, and this move screams 90s hockey. Powered by the success of the Detroit Red Wings and their hated rivals the Colorado Avalanche professional hockey had something of a renaissance in the nineties. This popularity also made Hollywood realize that movies about hockey would likely make them more money.

Some of those movies were done extremely well. Movies like *Mystery, Alaska* and *The Mighty Ducks* were extraordinarily well done, with the latter spawning two additional sequels and even Disney's own NHL expansion team in Anaheim. *Sudden Death…* is not in that same league.

While most people probably look at this movie and ask why in the world Jean-Claude would be leaving his kids alone at professional sporting event, I thought this was the most normal part of the movie. My uncle has worked for the NHL for most of my life, and when the Red Wings were not very successful at winning in the late 1980s, he had access to tickets for every game. Sometimes, when the tickets were unused, I would get a call as my uncle would be on his way to work and asked if I wanted to go. If my dad wasn't home or couldn't make it to the game, my uncle would take me to my seat and I would watch the game while he worked and he would come get me when the game was over. The first memory I have of this I was about nine or ten years old, so maybe the daughter being left alone is a bit much.

Speaking of the daughter, what kind of training has Jean-Claude been giving this girl? If I had seen a body with a bullet in its head at her age, I would have been catatonic. Throughout this movie, this young lady shows more fortitude than people 10 times her age. She is calm, rational, and quick-thinking. Even looking into the face of the big bad guy, this little girl tried to slap him and even marks him with her little stamper for easier identification later. When the bad guy finally gets his free ride to the afterlife on a helicopter crashing onto the ice, this little girl even glares at him as he burns in the wreckage. If anything goes down like this around me, I am calling this little girl to help before I would call Jean-Claude.

For some reason, I tend to watch a considerable number of political dramas. No idea why, but they just strike a chord with me. With that information, it makes the plot to take the Vice President hostage just makes my brain itch. Neither the President, nor the Vice President would enter a building of that size without the building being swept and secured for days in advance. The Vice President cannot be a surprise guest at a sporting event, for the reason displayed in this plot to take him hostage. Bombs planted, people replacing cleared individuals, single points of failure all over the place. On the upside, no one actually mentioned that "The United States does not negotiate with terrorists", so at least they didn't play that trope or this movie would have lasted about five minutes and ended with a giant explosion and mass casualties as opposed to the helicopter falling perfectly through the open roof of the stadium to the ice below.

Jean-Claude plays one of his more subdued characters in this movie. A firefighter that has lost his nerve after trying unsuccessfully to save a young girl in a collapsing building. He now works as a fire inspector and has the great fortune to be the inspector for game seven. This scores him a couple tickets and he decides to surprise his kids with the tickets. As it is the son's birthday and plans had already been made, this does not make Jean-Claude's ex-wife very happy though her new husband seems to be very complimentary of JC and helps to get Mom to allow the kids to go. If that woman is anything like the daughter she is raising, I would not want to be that new husband after everyone leaves.

One of the things I really like about this movie is that the effects and fight scenes are not over-done. Obviously, there is campiness, but it doesn't wear on me like it usually does. At face value, I would have expected at least one person to have their throat slashed by a skate, a chase across the ice, and for Van Damme to do the splits on top of net. None of those things happened! A guy did get his hand smashed with some form of pneumatic tool in the locker room, and he was the same guy that got a hockey stick across the throat, but honestly the unique ways of killing bad guys that these types of movies are known for was not on display here. Though JCVD's patented kicks did play heavily in the fight scenes as usual. The effects were pretty straight-forward for the most part, but the final scene where a helicopter rotates vertically and threads its way through the open roof of a hockey arena in order to have the main bad guy get smashed and blown up on the ice surface around which all the action has occurred throughout the movie. Great poetic license.

This movie may be standard action movie fare, but it is still one of my favorite action movies. Between it being based in a hockey arena, the solid special effects, and the most savage little girl you have ever seen it checks a lot of the boxes for re-watchability for me.

- Pat Kawula

Friends – "The One after the Superbowl, Part 2" (1996)

Super Bowl 30 has the distinction of being the lead-in game for the highest rated *Super Bowl* lead-out program of all time: Season 2, episodes 12/13 of the already popular show *Friends.* In what was an attempt for NBC to garner the highest grossing ad-revenue day since the beginning of the dawn of time…or at least the invention of television.

The now iconic show was still in its relative infancy, so while it wasn't exactly a gamble to premiere episodes after the Super Bowl, traditionally the biggest day for commercials and advertising already, the execs still thought it necessary to promote these episodes with a smattering of big-name celebrities.

These guest appearances differed in quality, for sure, and the episodes were panned by a lot of critics for the way they were wedged into the Friends preexisting format; arguably somewhat detached from the rest of the series in terms of tone and character consistency.

By far the most praised performance came from one of several casted icons, Brooke Shields, who proved herself to be a worthy comedienne with her portrayal of an off-the-wall soap opera fanatic who believes that Joey (Matt LeBlanc) is really the character of Dr. Drake Ramoray. Shields did such a credible (and funny) job that it landed her a sitcom pilot of her own, "Suddenly Susan".

Julia Roberts, Chris Isaak, Fred Willard, and Dan Castellaneta also show up at various points. Our subject here, one Mr. Jean-Claude Van Damme, played himself…as a sorta slimy version of himself who brushes aside Monica (Courtney Cox) and her flirty advances in order to try to pick up her pal Rachel (Jennifer Aniston). Of note, this is the only time that JCVD, Homer Simpson (Castellaneta), and Winnie the Pooh (who is voiced by another guest star, legendary Jim Cummings) ever appeared onscreen together.

So…I guess the question is, how did JC do?

Well, he didn't get a lot to work with, admittedly, alluded to earlier. He mostly just has to spout creepy lines and act like a smarmy handsome dude. His comic timing isn't the focus of the show, though he seemed to be game to try whatever they wanted him to do, and the results are effective, if not illuminating. In other words, he was ok.

He didn't get a sitcom spinoff from it, but he did alright.

The film *JCVD* did give him a chance to flex his comic muscles, and the results there were wonderful. In Friends, even though he doesn't have to deliver a ton of lines or kick anyone's ass, he still manages to display a certain amount of star power. Whatever it is that makes someone stand out, the charisma and the spark, he seems to have it.

Others were less forgiving to his work on the show, and he was singled out among the big cast by a lot of critics as being the stand-out in a different, unfortunate way: that he was the worst of the celeb guests. In retrospect, I probably agree with that, since Shields was great, Willard was his usual genius self, and Julia Roberts, despite being embroiled in a really goofy and infinitely unlikely subplot, played her part well.

Some even called JCVD's turn 'embarrassing' and compared the overall effect as being like a bizarre episode of *The Love Boat*, with recognizable faces appearing all over the place for little or no plot related reason.

In some small defense of our buddy Jean-Claude, maybe the writers did not know what to do with him. Shields and Roberts appear to have been given much more to sink their teeth into in terms of their roles, with their strengths being played up and some hilarious lines given to each (despite a pretty…well…*dumb* script). JCVD, on the other hand, mostly preens, acts cocky, and delivers his lines like he just heard them for the first time right before the director rolled camera. Worse, arguably, the show happens around him. He is almost nothing more than a prop for Monica and Rachel to play off, ultimately, not doing anything memorable enough to highlight any particular piece of his performance as being particularly funny or *good*.

The REAL story here is how reportedly unpopular he was on the set for the shoot. He was said to have been "ridiculously" late for filming his scenes, and by that we're talking a Joan Crawford-like TWELVE HOURS kind of late, at least according to *Generation Friends* author Saul Austerlitz.

TWELVE HOURS. That's a full sleep cycle plus three or four hours into a day that may have already included breakfast AND lunch. 12 hours is a shift and a half for a factory job. It's enough time to watch ALL THREE extended edition cuts of Peter Jackson's *Lord of the Rings* trilogy…and we are talkin' comfortably too, with time enough to spare for getting popcorn, whipping up a drink, and using the bathroom at a relatively relaxed rate between each flick.

Having Van Damme in the episodes was likely at least a tiny boost for the ratings, probably, since a lot of football fans who normally might have turned off *Friends* may have stuck around to see one of their action heroes do comedy, or at least be drawn in by the curiosity of his appearance. But still, *TWELVE HOURS*?

It's debatable whether or not his inclusion was worth all of the on-set turmoil that supposedly occurred during filming, but it becomes even more of a tougher defense to make when you take into consideration that the cast and crew had to wait for twelve hours to hear Jean-Claude Van Damme deliver the immortal line, "I can crush a walnut with my butt."

- Paul Counelis

The Quest (1996)

"This is the true story of a lost young man who started life with a gift, and through the grace of The Universe was given a Quest."

So begins the leather-bound prop book, *The Quest* by Carrie Newton, that appears in the closing moments of Jean-Claude Van Damme's directorial debut of the same name. The book is a superfluous, retrofitted framing device for the story just relayed first-hand by an aged Christopher Dubois. Van Damme portrays the protagonist himself, whom we follow from the streets of 1920's New York to The Lost City of Tibet, where he fights in the clandestine martial arts tournament known as the Ghan-gheng. The next paragraph of Newton's account ought to further detail Dubois' great journey but instead goes on to announce a new line of sailing and racing Genoese yachts. The filmmakers never replaced the template text in the design! Such is the attention to detail on display in the preceding 90-minute feature, a few cliched lines padded with the artifice of grandeur.

The title of this film has more to do with its creator than its content. Known to collectors of his early 90's appearances in magazines like *Karate International* and *Inside Kung-Fu* as everything from "Kumite" to "Enter The New Dragon," the movie that would become *The Quest* was to be Van Damme's grand salute to the genre that brought him worldwide fame and success before he went on to bigger and better things. By 1995, JCVD was at the peak of his powers in Hollywood, and he used that clout to write, star, and direct his dream project. Unfortunately, by the time *The Quest* hit theaters, the karate film conventions Van Damme helped define were already passé and offering only diminishing returns. It didn't help that the movie was more focused on slow-motion close-ups of its star actor/director and his famous "Muscles from Brussels" than its characters or story.

As early as 1991, Van Damme was quoted in everything from martial arts magazines to *The Washington Post* talking about his plans to someday make, "the biggest karate movie ever! [It's going to be] "like *Spartacus* in Tibet! We're going to open this movie at the Cannes festival in three years with the London Philharmonic!"

Recalling the inception of the film, Van Damme could almost be talking about his own experience coming to America from Belgium on a quest to be a movie star. "I was in a Thai restaurant. I was alone—maybe lonely—and I was drinking one or two beers, so I was kind of loose. And I started to write a story about an orphan—a guy who came from France on his own with a dream to become successful."

It's clear Van Damme's passion and dreams were the inspiration for *The Quest*, but they're not effectively channeled through the film itself. The driving force of *The Quest* should be the character of Christopher Dubois, but instead, it was the career aspirations of its auteur. Van Damme wanted his directorial debut to make Hollywood history, but he was too focused on being "the biggest" and lost sight of being "the best."

Back then, all of Van Damme's films were vehicles for his unique blend of karate and charisma. With each movie he was trying something new—even playing two characters in one film to show more versatility, all to make it onto Hollywood's A-List. In *The Quest*, he tries to cram too many character types into one role. Dubois is shown as a frail old man, a boyish man-child on stilts wearing mime makeup, a bearded stowaway, a chiseled Muay Thai champion, an impeccably dressed valet, and the only Ghan-ghen combatant not wearing a garish cartoon costume.

Even though they were rougher around the edges in terms of scope and industry respectability, most of Van Damme's pre-*Quest* films were filled with vigor and transcendence. The movies themselves may have been viewed as second-class, but his presence always elevated them. *The Quest* seems to be an attempt at combining elements of nascent, low-budget triumphs like *Bloodsport, Kickboxer*, and *Lionheart* with a Universal Pictures bankroll and the prestigious backdrop of a period film. Unfortunately, it lacks the focus and vitality of those earlier efforts.

The specious plot details and convoluted story of *The Quest* are secondary to the heroic exaltation ofVan Damme's character and pale in comparison to the simpler, more memorable execution in his previous films—*Bloodsport*, in particular. In both movies, there's the indomitable white American fighter with a thick European accent. There's "a secret contest where the world's greatest warriors fight in a battle to the death" (the actual tagline on the poster for *Bloodsport*). There's an opening credits montage in which invitations are delivered to the different fighters in their respective countries—all previewing their distinct styles—finishing with a surly American brawler who will become Van Damme's loyal friend. There's a scene where his character playfully evades pursuit by authorities, grinning ear to ear. There's a match-ending punch to the groin. There's a scene in which the fighter we're meant to think no one can beat kills a fellow tournament combatant in the ring to cement his status as The Big Bad. There's the slow-motion, knock-out "helicopter kick" to the face of Big Bad. And through it all, there's a tenacious blonde reporter after, "what every woman wants, a great story." (Those are words spoken out-loud in a major motion picture by an actress in *The Quest*!)

Whenever Van Damme talked about *The Quest*, the word "dream" was invoked, and the movie unfolds with something of a dream-like logic. At the beginning of the film, Dubois clutches a bag of money he has stolen from the mob and says to his gang of homeless street kids, "With this we buy respect. If we want something, we take it. Forever and ever." That's actual dialog a 32-year-old actor says to a gathering of children dressed like extras from *Newsies*. With money, they could buy things and no longer have to steal them! "Forever and ever"? This mashup of *Oliver!*, *Robinhood*, and *Peter Pan* is truly a bizarre puzzling preamble to the Kumite tournament promised in the opening credit sequence.

"The Kids," as he always refers to them, are just a vague, emotionally disconnected means of lending Van Damme's character a sense of nobility—the thief with a heart of gold… who later assumes a quest to steal a gold dragon. But Dubois never reveals why he wants the golden dragon. He hops aboard a ship to escape the mob and ends up on Muay Thai Island, so presumably, he wants it so he can pay his way back to New York and "The Kids," but he never says so. After the 30-minute mark, they're not referred to at all until the very end.

Predictably, Dubois wins the tournament, but he isn't awarded the golden dragon. Before the final match, he offers to forego the prize in exchange for the freedom of the men who sold him into slavery during the first act. These last few sentences may read like nonsequiturs, but it all makes about as much sense in the film. Just as with "The Kids," this sacrifice only serves to make Van Damme's character appear admirable.

When he is named the "greatest warrior of the Ghan-gheng," Chris smiles, puts on his newsboy cap, and saddles up to Carrie Newton. The two of them walk off to fulfill a romance barely hinted at as the golden dragon MacGuffin takes the foreground and Old Man Van Damme returns in voice-over to say, "I didn't get the golden dragon, but I returned to New York like I promised, got the kids off the streets... in the end, we all did just fine." How did he get the kids off the streets?! How is his situation any different now than it was when he fled?

The Quest raises innumerable unanswered questions—including the one which prompts the telling of the story-within-a-story-within-a-book in the film's first scene. After Old Man Van Damme rescues a bartender from being robbed with a few well-placed kicks and clever use of his cane, the man asks, "Where did you learn to fight like that?" Though Chris begins by replying "it was long ago..." there is never a training sequence. From the jump, whether he's kicking mobsters while juggling on stilts, besting bullies on Muay Thai Island, or fighting his way through a ship deck full of pirates, he is instantly sized up as Roger Moore's character as "the best fighter I've ever seen." (That's right, Sir Roger Moore is in this movie! But that's a whole other thing…)

Perhaps Chris's quest is one of character—to act honorably instead of the "what we want, we take" attitude with which he starts the film. The problem is, from the first frame he is always presented as a hero, so his redemption rings hollow.

Perhaps there's a truly epic two-and-a-half-hour cut of *The Quest* where everything is better set up and paid off, but what made it to the silver screen is mostly beauty shots of Van Damme and loosely associated sequences offering him a chance to act out the sorts of scenes he must have fantasized playing as a kid himself. In a wistful on-set interview, Van Damme describes the film as, "about a dream... about adventure... It's very epic. It has so many faces and corners, it has the shape of a diamond. That's my definition of *The Quest*."

Sadly, by the time he was promoting the film's release, Van Damme's dreams had gone bad. Struggling with drug addiction, marital problems, and the trappings of the status and fame he fought so hard for, the scrawny Belgian kid turned heavy-weight international action-movie superstar had even lost his desire to direct films.

"It was a nightmare," he continues in interview clips from *The Quest* press junket. "A movie take[s] a lot from you. It can drain everything you have. For four months, [I was working] six or seven days a week [...] sleeping three-to-four hours a day. To be able to be strong, physically in shape, long hours of shooting... I will not do it again. It was too hard. Ugh!"

It would be almost 15 years before Van Damme threw his newsboy cap in the ring as a director again. His follow-up to *The Quest* has yet to be commercially released, but it has been screened for distributors as *The Eagle Path* in 2010, *Soldiers* in 2012, and *Full Love* in 2014. In all incarnations of this unreleased opus, Van Damme plays Frenchy, a man "haunted by his past and determined to complete one last mission: His Own." Choking back tears on the 2011 reality TV series *Behind Closed Doors*, he admits, "in the editing room I thought about myself a little too much... of how to look the best... handsome... and this and that... and maybe didn't take too much care of the message."

The same could be said of *The Quest*, a movie also marred by vanity and hubris. Though still, despite all his faults, I can't help but root for the guy. In June of 2020, Van Damme declared the newly re-edited and re-named *Frenchy* "finally finished" and awaiting distribution. My take on *The Quest* may seem harsh, but that's only because I believe in Jean-Claude Van Damme. When he strikes the right balance—be it between two chairs, two Volvo trucks, or just among his better angels—he's every bit as great as *The Quest* aspires to be. And when *Frenchy* is eventually released, I'll be first standing in line—or logging online—to see it.

- David Ullman

Maximum Risk (1996)

This movie is quick to get to the action. Two minutes in, Van Damme has broken a door, collided with someone on the stairs, and created a ruckus in a street. It's a typical 90's action movie opener, I can't tell if I have missed those beginnings or not, but in the age of character depth, long run times, and more complicated plots, this little re-fresher was nice.

The plot of the movie is pretty much straight forward. Jean-Claude plays two people, identical twins, again, five years after *Double Impact*, this time he plays a cop and a Russian mobster. The Russian mobster is killed in the beginning and the cop needs to find out why.

Some of the early action in this movie is as entertaining now as it was when it was produced in 1996. It was awesome seeing JCVD throw a man in a burning building to the pointthat the individual catches on fire. The only thing that ruined that scene, was the over acting ofthe hostage.

Van Damme quickly travels to New York where he meets the chattiest cab driver in thehistory of film (don't hold me to that, it just felt like it) and the cab driver claims that since he isin the most powerful position in NYC, he can be an asset to helping Van Damme find what he is looking for. Van Damme, knowing the individual for just minutes, and being annoyed by him the whole time, decides hey go for it, and gives him the name of an individual to find.

It does get a little slow when he is trying to actually find who killed his brother. A scenetakes place outside where some street thugs try to intimidate Van Damme, but nothing happens (no ass kicking) because Van Damme is a cop. He is a cop with morals and doesn't want to fight anyone who has nothing to do with his brother's death.

He runs into his brother's girlfriend, who without hesitation, accepts that he is his brother (which I found to be unrealistic) and it's played off in the scene with Van Damme not saying a word, which normally I would find humorous, he did play confused really well in thescene. It does do a good job of creating a mystery to be solved.

The main villain Ivan, played by Zach Grenier is a Russian mobster, and to my surprise pulls it off well. He does have a thankless job of playing a villain who is not that interesting andto be honest, not that intimidating when put next to Van Damme.

I wish the plot was interesting. The action scenes started off great, but quickly fizzled out. The cab driver, whose main job was to function as comedic relief, just became annoying. I dreaded each time Van Damme got into a cab. The dialogue isn't bad, it's just generic, there are no quotable lines, just stuff for people to say. I feel like the writer was going for a motif of some kind dealing with reflections, since the movie deals with twins, however what the writer was going for, if he was going for anything, was lost on me. The final battle features a scene where a man is shot holding a chainsaw and he falls to the ground as he continues to chainsaw some meat in half, maybe the writer wrote that to handle the theme of separation, or maybe I am just trying to give this movie any ounce of credit I can. Larry Ferguson, wrote this movie, who actually wrote or co-wrote some of the biggest movies of the early 90's like *The Hunt for Red October* and *Alien 3*, his career came to a sudden halt when he wrote the remake to *Rollerball* and that movie tanked.

Maximum Risk was directed by Ringo Lam, who would go on to work with Van Dammeagain for *In Hell.* He does the typical 90's movie action direction of being long and drawn out when it comes to action sequences and quick with the plot devices. Natasha Henstridge struggles with her character, trying to be more than eye candy, but isn't. She falls trap to the same basic plot points as all women in the 90's action films. Does she fall quickly for the male lead? Check. Does she scream at the first sign of danger? Check. Does she get kidnapped or held hostage, which leads to the protagonist rescuing her? Check. Shows breasts? Check.

Van Damme does the best he can with a story that gets more boring the longer it continues. The other films I have reviewed have been good or at least interesting. This is a film I have on when I can't sleep at night. I am going to add this movie to that list right now. His action sequences entertain. The sounds of bones breaking never gets old in an action movie, at least in my opinion. Van Damme does nothing that sways the vote from good or bad at all. His line deliveries aren't bad, his acting gets the job done, it was just not that interesting to watch. This movie has a real "product feel" where the studios made a movie, casted, filmed, edited, and released, and then forgotten about especially since it just made it money back, withthe help of foreign markets. It is one of Van Damme's forgotten films. It's not that it's a bad film,it was just a down the line, run of the mill picture, that would show up on clearance bins or put with a compilation of other films of similar nature. I have been entertained by Van Damme and I have laughed at wrong times because of his portrayals; I even sat through a Russian film with no subtitles and was more entertained with those films, this one was just boring. Van Damme has done better.

- Stephen Kessen

Double Team (1997)

When thinking about the Van Damme/Dennis Rodman epic that is called *Double Team*, I realized that I had seen the film exactly one time, when it was originally released on home video via a rental (at one of those little local video rental places from a bygone era – I think it was called Panorama Video? But that's a different story). For some reason whenever the movie came up in conversation or if I thought about it (not very often), I would think of the title as having been *Rebound*, which is the title of a completely different, equally bad movie starring Martin Lawrence (and another movie, a decent Don Cheadle flick about basketball legend Earl "The Goat" Manigault).

The biggest difference between Martin's film and this one is that Martin's is just a bad flick, and *Double Team* is DEFINITELY a "so bad it's good" all-star film. From the title on (which might illicit a giggle or two from some of the cruder folk among us – hey, at least they didn't call it *Tip Off*), as soon as this movie starts you know you are in for a good, weird time. REALLY weird.

This movie is about blah blah blah plutonium and a special scary bad guy, wherein JCVD faces off with hilarious action film dialogue delivered in hammy, stilted fashion, "Come on, Jack…this is your last shot. Face it, Jack…you can't retire until *he* does."

The "he" in this instance is none other than Mickey Rourke, and man… he is super game to be the weirdest action villain we've seen in a while. I shit you not. He is odd. That is, until we are introduced to basketball star Rodman, who will clearly be wrestling ol' Mickey for the title of "strangest character in this movie".

Of course, as soon as our hero JCVD meets Rodman, he's getting a tattoo while wearing the most unusual attempt at a shirt that I can recall seeing in some time. He has black streaks in his blond hair, and he is fiddling with a belly button ring with his multi-colored fingernails.

Of course, because this is one of those vaunted "Movies for guys who like movies", we IMMEDIATELY get a dad hair joke, and it is an odd one. "Who does your hair, Siegfried or Roy?" To which Rodman woodenly replies, in a superlatively non-menacing attempt at menace, "The last guy who made fun of my hair…they're still trying to pull his head out of his ass." JC responds with, "I don't want to know about your sex life." Ho Ho.

And we're off and running.

Now listen, Mickey Rourke has given some damn good performances in some damn good movies, with some (like my pal, the poet Glen Birdsall) even comparing him (favorably) with Marlon Brando in a few roles. Let's be clear about something right up front: this is decidedly NOT one of those films. It is hard to say if this would rank as Rourke's *Island of Dr. Moreau*, since Mickey has been in several flat-out stinkers playing some weirdo mfers, but it *has* to be a contender.

We also meet JCVD's delta force team, and they seem formidable. In fact, the woman muses that she can "shoot the dick off a hummingbird", which is indeed a helluva brag…but hummingbirds don't actually have dicks, so a biology major she is not. Whatever. We get her "guys who like movies" implication, but she doesn't get the chance to prove it, because stealth, hammy baddie Rourke gets her while she's lining up a shot. Shame.

Luckily for Van Damme, Rourke's minions all shoot like stormtroopers, so JC is able to crawl all over amusement park rides and get away without a scratch. Rourke, however, who has taken grenades and semi-automatic weapons to the park on an outing with his young son, loses said son to the gunfire (and to the fact that he tries to rescue the kid before all of the gunplay is finished). He goes crazy and starts shooting clowns and popcorn machines and stuffed animals and elephant ear.

But wait, we gotta go back, because the reason that Rourke is tipped off to JCVD and the hummingbird shooter's intentions is by looking at the eyes of a tiger in a cage next to the park rides. When Mickey glances over at the tiger, the animal looks up toward the location where the good guys are hiding. Yes, for real. Now, had the title been *Tip Off*, this could have been the moment where we went, "OH, *there* it is."

The reason we're spending so much time talking about the amusement park scene is because it's just so gloriously epic. As tons of people are tossin' out grenades and shooting up the park, a lot of people are paying it no mind and continue to sit calmly while their rides run, or others play games or get food, and still others just hang out seemingly oblivious to the devastation going on around them. LITERALLY around them, in some cases, as in one instance Rourke scales the side of a ride filled with dozens of people, a couple of whom admittedly react a little.

Before we get back to the cinematic pork that is Dennis Rodman, we have to sit through a super boring segment where everyone sits around some screens (*Star Wars* senate style) and examine satellite images and talk about guy movie shit like 'interlocking lasers'. But it is worth it (depending on the way you look at it), because we also get an incredible scene where Van Damme is working out using a water filled bathtub as a weight.

No, I didn't make that up. He is doing squats with a bathtub.

He's also conducting fingerprinting experiments with Coke cans and erasers and other MacGyver type stuff to prepare for his showdown. And when he shows up again to see Rodman, we can see that the bathtub lifting has paid off...he is able to stop Rodman's motorcycle by lifting the back end. Yup.

A lot crazier stuff happens, and Rodman wears amazing suspender shirts, and Mickey chews more scenery, and Dennis and Jean-Claude sky dive with basketball reference jokes like "Now, that's what I call 'hang time'".

I *think* they resolve the plutonium issue or whatever, but for some reason *Double Team* never got a sequel. *Double Team 2: Nothing But Net* was not to be.

- Paul Counelis

Knock Off (1998)

Ask any Jean-Claude Van Damme fan for their favourite JCVD movie and you'll probably hear *Bloodsport* every time. But ask for their second favourite and you might get a different title back from everyone you ask. You might hear *Hard Target*, *Lionheart* or *Replicant*, pretty much anything except *Street Fighter*. From me, you'd hear *Knock Off* without a second thought.

This is a Hong Kong action movie, directed by the legendary Tsui Hark and with cinematography by the legendary Arthur Wong—winner of three consecutive Hong Kong Film Awards *on three separate occasions.* It feels like golden age Jackie Chan, right down to the recognisable humour. No, it's not *Project A*, *Wheels on Meals* or *Armour of God*, but it's not unfair to put it in their company. It's full of quintessentially Hong Kong stunt work, explosions and fight scenes, and it enjoys the quirky local culture. And yes, it seems strange to suggest all this, given that Van Damme's co-star is, well, Rob Schneider.

I'm not sure what their characters really do, as it surely isn't the fashion design synopses usually suggest. As Tommy Hendricks, Schneider certainly runs a fashion show in Hong Kong for his American client, V-Six Jeans. As Marcus Ray, Van Damme is certainly tied up in counterfeit production, half their last shipment to the U.S. being cheap knockoffs. But are they designers? Who knows? And who really cares, when they spend most of their time being idiots and not only in an annual charity race? Schneider whipping JCVD with an eel is surely worth the price of admission all on its own.

I should mention that *Knock Off* begins like a Japanese version of *Charlie's Angels*. Frogmen find a crate of dolls in the sea, knock-off dolls that are wired to explode so that the sea soon looks like a 4th July fireworks display. One cop chases the Russian villains in a boat, but only nabs a corpse with a grenade underneath it. Something serious is happening and it's clearly tied to the counterfeit market but, by the time we get to the race, we don't care.

It's a rickshaw street race, so Van Damme is on foot, in knock-off trainers which quickly fall apart, and Schneider is sitting in the rickshaw his partner is hauling for the V-Six team. It's glorious fun, with copious amounts of cheating and big money bet on the winner. Well, it's fun for us watching but less fun for Hendricks and Ray, who have to deal not only with cheating teams and giant stone steps but the kidnapping of a competitor and soon a murder, the destruction of an entire grocery store and the arrest of both of them.

The character kidnapped is Eddie Wang, who's family to Marcus, as well as one of the leading lights in the counterfeit production industry, so you can see how our heroes get caught up in the broader story. You can't see all of it, because I'm withholding a lot of crucial information, but you have enough. This isn't just about knockoffs; it's about miniaturised explosives that the Russians have got down to the size of a watch battery, designed to be detonated remotely. And it's also about the return of Hong Kong to Chinese rule, as everything that happens here does so during the build-up to the handover ceremony.

Van Damme clearly had a blast making this movie. In an American film, he'd be Schneider's straight man, but this is Hong Kong, so they're both wacky and he's obviously enjoying it, their dumb grins sometimes reminding me of Bill and Ted. Marcus rips one of Tommy's shirts by flexing his muscles and the nanobombs make a cheap excuse to have him strip to his undies. Streetwise and tough, however much he sings along to Cantopop, he gets plenty of opportunity to fight in ever more-outrageous Hong Kong choreography using whatever props he can find to hand. One memorable battle has him take on a machete-armed gang by wrapping chains around his arms.

I love pretty much everything about this movie, even the abundant technical gimmickry with cameras placed in strange locations; zooms in split screen and up guns about to fire; pauses for effect and both slowed down and sped up film; even CGI shots following bullets through walls or electronic bits through circuitry, like from one mobile phone to another.

I love the explosions, which start big and only get bigger, and I love the green fire that adds an extra dimension to them. I love the chases, which often include fights and explosions too. I love the wackiness, which can get a little much in Hong Kong movies but stays enjoyable here. I love the layers of plot that complicate the story in agreeable ways; the core of it is counterfeits, so it's appropriate for many of the characters to not be who they say they are either. I love the good old-fashioned *Doc Savage*-style karma-fuelled ending.

I particularly love that rickshaw race, especially given that its payoff introduces Carman Lee as a Hong Kong policewoman; never mind all the plot conveniences, my biggest problem with this film was that I wanted a lot more screen time for her.

And, of course, I love the stunt work. It's there throughout the movie, getting progressively more insane, up to an amazing action scene at sea. The good guys fight the bad guys on a ship amidst moving cargo containers and the precision of the stunt work is impeccable. The fights, and especially the stunts, feel dangerous in the way that they so rarely do in Hollywood and JCVD was obviously at the heart of both. There's a scene in that container battle where he's a fraction of a second away from being crushed to death. I'm sure he wasn't, even knowing how many people get hurt in Hong Kong movies, but it sure looked like it! *Bloodsport* is more iconic, I'll grant you, but *Knock Off* is way more batshit crazy fun.

- Hal CF Astell

Legionnaire (1998)

Obviously, I'm going to bash the shit out of this universally panned movie, right? But you know what? I really, really like this film. It gets big points with me for its perhaps ridiculous (but admirable) aspirations to be some giant epic on par with *Lawrence of Arabia*. It's most assuredly not that, but it's wildly entertaining and Jean-Claude Van Damme, whose English-speaking performances have generally been about as wooden as a scarecrow's dick, is pretty decent here. I'm not saying he's Robert De Niro or Laurence Olivier or anything, but he's decent in a way that doesn't make you want to make fun of him and that's something in itself.

The film was co-written by Van Damme, Rebecca Morrison, and Sheldon Lettich, who most notably wrote *Bloodsport*, which is probably the best of the Van Damme actioners. Lettich is a craftsman in a genre in which craftsmen aren't allowed. Artistry is not highly regarded in the action film world. *Legionnaire* was directed by Peter MacDonald, a noted cinematographer whose biggest directorial credit is *Rambo III*. Van Damme and company clearly wanted to make a film that transcended the action genre—a "real" movie with real merit. They may well have accomplished that had the film been directed by a more talented director. MacDonald isn't a hack by any means, but he's also not a filmmaker with a style you might confuse for being David Lean's. MacDonald's direction is fine for run-of-the-mill actioners but not for something wanting to be epic.

We've discussed Van Damme, so now let's discuss some of his co-stars. Steven Berkoff, an actor known for playing baddies in such films as *Octopussy*, *Rambo: First Blood Part II*, and *Beverly Hills Cop*, of course plays a character written for the audience to hate, and he does a fine job, as always. Adewale Akinnuoye-Agbaje, best known for playing the character Adebisi on the 1990s HBO series *Oz*, turns in a nice performance here as the lone Black Foreign Legionnaire. Nicholas Farrell, the English actor who plays Van Damme's buddy Mackintosh also does very nice work.

The film looks great, which should be no surprise since it's directed by a cinematographer. One problem might be that it seems to have been made in the wrong era. *Saving Private Ryan* was made the same year *Legionnaire* was made, and *Saving Private Ryan* significantly raised the bar for what a war movie was supposed to look like. It was bleak and gory and damning of war, whereas *Legionnaire* is a throwback to a time when war movies focused on heroism. *Legionnaire* never feels like it's anti-war, but then it never really tells us anything about why the French are battling the Berbers in Morocco or even how the Legionnaires feel about this. It's a pretty one-dimensional film, despite its epic aspirations. Despite its deficiencies, however, it's a good-looking, adequately acted film. The dialogue never feels clunky or action-movie-y with Schwarzenegger-style one-liners. The script is actually pretty decent.

If there are any complaints to make about the script, it's that it's story feels like it was lifted from a number of classic Hollywood films. It's too familiar. There's the boxer (Van Damme) who agrees to take a dive for the mob boss but doesn't. There's also the man (also Van Damme) who plans to run away with the mob boss' moll. And the backstory of the boxer and the moll is sort of a low-rent *Casablanca* with the two lovers head-over-heels for each other and planning to meet at the airport and one of them not showing up. (Why don't these people ever just go to the airport together?) Then, once all of this happened, the story becomes *Beau Geste* with Van Damme running away and joining the French Foreign Legion. There's certainly nothing wrong with reusing elements from classic films. I mean, look at Quentin Tarantino. The only thing is, that works for Tarantino because when he lifts something he adds significantly to it to make something that's better than the original. And there's no candy-coating this aspect of it—no matter how much I may like *Legionnaire*, and I do, it does nothing to improve on any of the classic tropes it reuses.

The story does take an interesting turn when two of the mob boss' goons enlist in the French Foreign Legion to kill Van Damme's character, somehow (unbelievably) ending up assigned to the same fort as their target. This setup promises to yield some really interesting turns of events, but it fails to fully capitalize on the promise. There is a small "twist" when the bad guys persuade one of Van Damme's buddies to turn on him, but then it ends up going exactly the way you think it will—the buddy saves Van Damme at the moment of the truth. Again, I don't believe these things ruin the movie, but all of the good elements feel like they have a lot of promise that they just never seem to be able to fully deliver on. And speaking of the fort where all the soldiers are being killed, all of that seems extremely reminiscent of *The Alamo*... And that's fitting because *Legionnaire* feels very much like a John Wayne movie with Jean-Claude Van Damme instead of the Duke. And as much as you might argue that John Wayne couldn't act, he was a far better actor than Van Damme.

In closing, *Legionnaire* is a far better movie than it has any right to be since it's a Van Damme movie directed by the helmer of *Rambo III*, but it comes so close to actually being good that it'll break your heart. It's not the terrible movie critics will have you believing it is, but it's also not the great movie it could have been. It's just good, which for a Van Damme movie is more than enough.

- Andrew J. Rausch

Universal Soldier: The Return (1998)

One of the first images of this movie is a man standing up, facing down, with his arms spread open like he is about to give up, and after seeing this movie, he probably should have. It then shows credits in the style of a computer program with the green letters, which after seeing the traditional white letters that fade over the movie, it is a nice change of pace for a little while, but then it gets annoying because you are just watching names.

It quickly gets into action mode with Van Damme on a jet ski shooting at people. It quickly shows that this is a training exercise, which I am still trying to figure because they used live ammunition and I get it, they are genetically altered soldiers so they can tolerate a lot more, but it still seems stupid, how do you train something that is essentially invincible. I get five minutes into this mercifully 82-minute movie, and I am already finding logic problems. The 82 minutes felt like days.

Things quickly get going when a soldier "gets hacked" and goes after people in the lab. I laughed because Van Damme is grabbed and lifted up, he quickly looks at the computer screen to see where he can hit the soldier and then he goes about his day as if nothing as happened. It also features a cyber babysitter named S.E.T.H, who we are introduced to when he babysits Van Damme's daughter (the best an operating system can). Immediately after this scene, we are force fed so much exposition for those who didn't see the first movie, which explains how the government views the program.

S.E.T.H (Self-Evolving Thought Helix) eventually finds out that the government wants to shut down the program and disagrees with the idea to the point that he takes over the minds of the universal soldiers, Van

Damme is not considered a universal soldier due to a medical procedure where he is now just a regular individual. S.E.T.H goes on to be played by Michael Jai White when he implants himself into that body. S.E.T.H shuts down the lab and traps individuals inside. He quickly turns the universal soldiers against the humans.

The direction of this is almost laughably bad. Mic Rodgers directed this film and as of 2020, this is the only film he has directed. He is known in the stunt world for his work there on films like *12 Strong, Bird Box*, and *Hacksaw Ridge* (he was Mel Gibson's personal stunt double for several years.) It shows why he only directed one film: he is not a director. He has little sense of camera style, proper exposition, or general direction.

One scene involves Van Damme's partner Maggie (played by Kiana Tom) attacking Bill Goldberg (yes, the professional wrestler) and she succeeds in knocking him down (it's bullshit) and then she rides him down the stairs like a damn jet ski. I laughed hard at that scene.

The writing of this film is also terrible. I get the idea of the machines eventually taking over, however T2: Terminator 2: Judgement Day handled that theme with so much more grace. The lines of dialogue are so on-the-nose, I felt like it was a college project with an absurdly high budget. If you want to have a fun drinking game of this movie, take a shot every time someone asks what is going on despite Van Damme explaining that S.E.T.H has taken over. I love Bill Goldberg getting caught on fire and saying, "I'm just warming up." it's a line so stupid, I couldn't help but admire Goldberg's dedication to the delivery. I also love the scene where a woman punches an army general, and he just tolerates it. On a side note, there are other sequels in the Universal Soldier franchise, however they don't mind ignoring this entry to contradicting it. This film is considered by many to not be canon and for good reason, it sucks.

I also want to give a special shout out to the music selection to this film. The film was released in 1999 and it uses a lot of heavy metal music where you can only really understand 1/3 of the lyrics. There is no rhyme or reason to the soundtrack, the director just thinks that loud music and lots of violence makes a good movie. The audience gives a shit about the story, though.

Jean-Claude Van Damme does the best he can with almost every aspect of this film working against him. He does his best to look serious, but this movie is absurd. His acting is the best it can be when you have the dumbest lines of dialogue. Michael Jai White seems to be having fun playing S.E.T.H, the others are just there to help move the plot along. Jean doesn't get a chance to show off his martial arts skills here, instead he is given a big gun and told to go hunting. Bill Goldberg probably had fun fighting with Van Damme, but he exists to just fight and to provide some sort of emotional moment when he is hacked and turns against Van Damme.

I went in with the lowest expectations of this movie. I knew it wasn't going to be good when I fell asleep watching the original. It didn't provide me with much entertainment aside from the aforementioned riding of Goldberg down the stairs. If you want a good action movie, stay far away from this one. If you want background noise, also stay away from this movie. If you find yourself saying that you are too intelligent and need to kill some brain cells, then put this movie in and boy, will you lose some. I know I lost a few brain cells. I felt them pop.

- Stephen Kessen

Inferno (1999)

Inferno (aka *Desert Heat*) starts off with Eddie Lowmax (JCVD) riding his motorcycle in the desert being chased by a wolf. You quickly find out that Eddie is suicidal. He's a veteran who is tired of living. Six minutes in the movie, you will see Eddie beaten by a group of gang members. The group leaves Eddie for dead and that inspires Eddie to live and something to fight for. They didn't just nearly kill him; they took his prized motorcycle. Eddie doesn't like it when you leave him for dead and take his motorcycle. Eddie heals and quickly goes for revenge. He soon discovers gangs, women, and interesting towns people.

This movie was directed by John G Avildsen, yes, the same guy, who won the Academy Award for directing *Rocky*. I will forever wonder just who the hell he pissed off to go from *Rocky* to directing this B-movie. The last movie I found him directing was *8 Seconds*, so maybe he upset Stephen Baldwin or Luke Perry. I am surprised Avildsen agreed to direct this, however further research indicates that he was not happy with the film, as his credit is listed as Danny Mulroon. Avildsen gets some returning company like Pat Morita, who was Mr. Miyagi in *The Karate Kid* films, playing an ally of Eddie's who helps him get rid of the bodies. I think Avildsen called everyone who could help him and beg to make working on this movie tolerable.

The biggest problem I have with this movie is the story and how contradictory it seems to the goal of the protagonist. Eddie, as stated above, is a soldier battling PTSD. The souls of the people he has killed haunt him. He is nearly killed, which is something I think he would be thankful for, but then we would have a ten-minute movie. He goes on a hunt to get his motorcycle back, which makes me wonder if he thinks he can take his motorcycle with him in the afterlife. If he is haunted by the souls of the people he killed, it stands to reason he wouldn't want to kill more people. Eddie's friend Johnny Sixtoes (Danny Trejo) helps him through his recovery. It introduces him as a mirage first, then a real person. I will say that this is the only script written by Tim O'Rourke, which to me, shows that it was not well received. Most of the dialogue is laughable and when it's not, it's on the nose. There's an obligatory love interest, who falls for Eddie after his rescues her at a bar. The screenplay feels like it was written by creating a list of stock characters, putting them in a basic plot, giving them, what I'm sure felt like witty lines, and hoping all ends well. One scene that amused me is when women at the bar wanted to "thank" Eddie for helping them and he ends up with them. It's played for laughs, and it earns them. You can call the ending of the movie a mile away, sometimes that's not too bad provided the journey is a fun one. *Inferno* is not a fun journey, it's a boring one filled with things we have all seen before, with people who have done so much better. Did someone say let's take the talents of people in front of and behind the camera and make a crappy movie? If that was the case, they succeeded with flying colors.

Now let's get to the guest of honor, Jean-Claude Van-Damme. I don't have too many problems with his performance here. It's clear that the themes are the most focused part of this movie. He goes on a basic path of revenge to kill those who tried to kill him, when he was just trying to kill himself. It's hard to critique a performance when so much is working against it. He's doing the best he can, but as the movie continues, it seems to lose energy. I wish he was given a better script here He makes the best of a bad situation, but some scenes you can physically see the pain of having to play them a certain way. Here's where the trouble with Van-Damme starts; the film is listed as an action comedy, which makes sense, but did someone tell him that? I can't tell if he is purposely the straight man or if comedy makes him nervous to the point of not going for laughs and just saying the lines. If you want action from Van-Damme, there are so many other better movies for that. This was a paycheck movie. You get the kicks, the shootouts, the knife throws, but it just feels bland and uninteresting. It's like Avildsen told him to just "do what you do" and we will make it work.

There are many poorer performances than Van-Damme in *Inferno.* I couldn't tell the thugs apart after a while because there is no reason to care. A lot of the actors have to say terrible lines and I imagine there were plenty of fights over lines of dialogue. I can also imagine the actors huddling together and just agreeing to say the most generic action movie lines ever. I just wanted to see Eddie get his motorcycle back and I had to sit through a pedantic, uninteresting story to get there.

In conclusion, you can skip this movie, unless you are a teacher at a film school and you must torture your students in an unfathomable way. I would love to see a group of students watch this movie and point to where it went wrong. I would imagine you would get many different replies. I know Van-Damme is ripe for parody, but I felt a little pity for him this time.

- Stephen Kessen

"Crush 'em" (1999)

I remember hating Megadeth's "Crush 'em" music video when it first came out in 1999. While I wasn't a huge Megadeath fan, I did appreciate their music for what it was; crank it up and bang it out rock and roll. And I did actually enjoy Jean-Claude Van Damme's *Universal Solider: The Return*, where this song appeared. But I just couldn't dig the video, which had all the sincerity of a GI Joe toy commercial. But hey, that was 1999. I also remember liking "All Star" from Smash Mouth that year (don't judge me! Ok, maybe a little, but keep in mind, I was REALLY high for most of 1999). So, when I re-watched the video recently, I approached it with a "Time heals all wounds" attitude. Unfortunately, I think John Lennon's "Time wounds all heels" may be more fitting. Just like Smash Mouth still sucks, this does as well.

I realize I am being a bit harsh. The age of music videos was already over when this came out, but we were just too stupid (or REALLY high) to realize it then. So, in a lot of ways, this really needs to be judged as a movie trailer, because that's what it actually is, sans the "please quiet your cell phone" and "throw all trash in the receptacle" messaging that we ignored then and still do today. And when we do that…it still sucks.

It actually takes about 45 seconds to realize this isn't just a standard Megadeath video, as a low and pulsating bass line opens onto a scene of a dystopian…Amazon fulfillment center? Which would actually make sense. Nothing says the future is going to be shit than the prospect of working for $15 an hour retrieving endless orders of crotchless panties, protein shakes and camo unisex crocs. In fact, perhaps Jeff Bezos could take a hint from the Universal Solider franchise and use some of his Megawealth (see what I did there?) and actually create a UniSol program of his own. Just take the corpses of the Amazon employees who commit suicide and reanimate them as soulless tech workers called UniBezos. It would certainly be a better use of his money than penis-shaped rockets to take him and his dickhead friends to the edge of space so they can pee on the rest of us down below. But I digress.

As the video proceeds we see cutaways of the UniSols spliced in with shots of the band. We even catch a glimpse of Goldberg, who plays bad guy Romeo in the movie. But as you might imagine our first sighting of the man himself, JCVD, only occurs as front man Dave Mustaine hits the chorus:

Heads I win, tails you lose

Out of my way, I'm comin' through

Roll the dice, don't think twice

And we crush (crush), crush 'em (crush 'em)

Ok, Lord Byron he isn't. But now at least we have the gist of the story. Van Damme = good. Goldberg = bad. Who needs IMDb to sort this out? Not us.

But wait, there's more…of the same obligatory rotating shots of the singer, to the guitarist, to the bassist, to the drummer. Now to Goldberg. Back to Mustaine, now here's JCVD punching the camera. Now he's… wait for it…giving the camera a high kick…and he's broken the lens! I did not see that coming. I was sure the camera would win that one. Next time camera, next time.

So, the point is, it is predictable. Should that be a surprise? No, not really. It isn't a Fellini masterpiece for shit's sake; it's a fucking music video. I get that. But it could have been so much better. To prove that point, one need only watch the video Van Damme did with The Smithereens for 1994's cover of "Time Won't Let Me" that appeared on the *Timecop* soundtrack. That fully integrated Van Damme into the action, interspersed actual clips from the movie and most importantly, was entertaining to watch. The

"Crush em'" video has all the pizazz of a band warm up. And ultimately that's all anyone wants from these. I'm not expecting something worthy of a Cannes entry. Just fucking entertain me. Is that so much to ask for? In this case, the answer is yes.

- Jon Arking

Replicant (2001)

Sometimes you want a nice ham and cheese sandwich. You put two pieces of bread on a plate, slather on your condiment of choice, and then put on the ham. Finally, you reach in to the diary drawer, only to find that the cheddar has a fine patina of mold. At this point, some will abandon the sandwich and opt for something else for lunch. Others will scrape off the mold to get to the fine cheese beneath.

Replicant has some moldy spots, but you will be hard pressed to find a tastier block of cheese.

The main draw of the film is that you get twice the Van Dammeage for your ticket price. So, if you didn't get enough double JCVD in *Double Impact, Maximum Risk,* and *Timecop*, well here you are. In this outing, Van Damme plays Edward "The Torch" Garrotte, a serial killer who punishes what he perceives to be bad mothers. This punishment includes torture, murder, and setting the women on fire. He also plays the unnamed "Replicant" made from The Torch's DNA. The main cast is rounded out by Michael Rooker (pursuing the serial killer instead of being one this time around) as retired Detective Jake Riley and *The Shield*'s Catherine Dent as Angie, another detective.

Riley and crew almost catch The Torch in the opening action set piece, but the killer escapes. We then learn that Riley has not only been pursuing the killer for years, but The Torch has also been contacting him by phone after each kill. He calls during Riley's retirement party, leading to one of many explosive bursts of anger seen throughout the film. Riley is contacted by a shadowy government agency, and then things get a little weird.

The group has cloned The Torch, using science and stuff, and sped up his aging so the Replicant is, well, also able to be played by Jean-Claude. At this point they have a perfect duplicate of the killer, including his face, so they could simply plaster the media with his image. Instead, they give the Replicant to Riley because the new being will be exactly like the original and will lead the group right to the killer.

These scientists all fall heavily on the "nature" side of the "nature v nurture argument."

This is a little off, as the movie does reveal *why* The Torch has been killing — because of a traumatic event involving his mother scolding him and a fire. One of the most chilling scenes in the film involves The Torch confessing to his hospital bed bound mother his most recent kill.

Why the mother doesn't alert someone is ah, not discussed.

The Replicant is an odd mix of adult and isolated lump of clay with no background who may have a psychic connection with The Torch. Some of the best scenes involve the Replicant learning from his surroundings. He learns the pommel horse by watching a gymnast on television. He picks up his dialogue from what is said to him — most often from Riley, most often swear words.

He also learns fight choreography from the dozens of times he gets the crap beaten out of him. These are the best examples of the instant learning coded into his DNA. An agent tries to put him in an arm lock and a few moments later the same move is used on the agent but resulting in much more damage. There are a few showdowns between Van Damme's dual characters where they are throwing the same moves simultaneously which are brilliantly choreographed.

Riley takes the Replicant to the scenes of various murders. While there, the clone picks up images of what happened. Through these visits they are able to trace The Torch. Upon learning of his clone's existence, The Torch tries to get his "brother" to turn on Riley and come with him. There is never any real tension in these scenes, as we know that the Replicant is going to side with Riley, despite everything that has been done to him.

Which brings us to the primary negative aspect of the film. Riley's character is wildly volatile. In some scenes he is likable, almost nurturing when it comes to his charge. Then he turns around and beats the Replicant bloody. Quite honestly, it would make perfect sense for the Replicant to try and kill Riley, even if he never meant his DNA donor. Riley's treatment of the Replicant, at times, stems from the belief that he will eventually turn into another serial killer. The retired detective has no problem using him, however. Despite the occasional nice moment, Riley is a fairly unredeemable character, and the film might have been better off if he had died in the end.

Naturally, *Replicant* builds to a final showdown between the two Van Damme characters. There is the required melancholy self-sacrifice which we've all been expecting since the beginning, watered down by the "he might have survived" ending.

While *Replicant* is not high cinema by any means, it does have many things going for it. Van Damme does a good job playing two entirely different characters. The Torch has a menacing swagger and general bad-assery which is quite the opposite of the naive Replicant seeing the world for the first time. The action scenes are outstanding, as one would expect from the late Ringo Lam. If one is looking for fun escapist action and can swallow a healthy dose of suspension of disbelief during the opening credits, *Replicant* will satisfy.

- Michael Cieslak

The Order (2001)

You'd think that *The Order* ought to work well. It's a Jean-Claude Van Damme feature, released immediately after *Replicant*, and he co-wrote this too. He plays Rudy Cafmeyer, a playboy thief who lives for risky jobs such as stealing a Fabergé egg from the Russian mob, always with a cheeky grin on his face. It was directed by Sheldon Lettich, who had co-written *Bloodsport* and *Legionnaire* and directed *Lionheart* and *Double Impact*. It takes place predominantly in Israel, an agreeably unusual location for an action movie, but appropriate when we're dealing with a heretical religious order founded by an 11th century Christian knight, also played by Van Damme, who found his beliefs changed by his experiences during the First Crusade. Oh, and the co-star is Charlton Heston and the villain is Brian Thompson. How can all that go wrong?

Well, it does, quickly and often. It's not awful but it's very forgettable. The playboy thief angle is fun for a few scenes but is quickly forgotten. Lettich did much better with every other JCVD film he was involved with, even *Cyborg* and *The Quest*, where he did next to nothing. The locations are decent, but the whole Indiana Jones style plot featuring dubious religious mythology rapidly devolves into cheap sets and cheaper dialogue. And, while Thompson milks his one-dimensional character all he can, Heston vanishes from the movie about as quickly as we realised he was in it, murdered in Tel Aviv after a car chase.

Fortunately, there's a bright side. There's a sequence where Van Damme is chased on foot through the Old City of Jerusalem by the Israeli police while, get this, disguised as a Hasidic Jew. And yes, I know you double took but it's true. This is easily one of the most gloriously surreal sequences to be found anywhere in Van Damme's filmography, even if he's been trying to add some more lately, given *Jean-Claude Van Johnson* and *JCVD's Day Out*.

Prospective viewers would be advised to fast forward to this chase, enjoy the heck out of it and then drift away again. And I'll fill you in on what you'll miss.

That knight was Charles le Vaillaint and his life-changing epiphany was that it was dumb to kill people who believed in God in the name of God. He figured out that they were all worshipping the same one, even if they gave Him different names, so he formed an order for Christians, Muslims and Jews alike. He wrote his thinking down too and might have changed the world, had not he and his disciples been massacred on the way to Syria by his old Crusader buddies, leaving the final chapter of his magnum opus lost in the desert.

Fast forward to New York City in the present, where Rudy's dad, Ozzie Cafmeyer, has that lost final chapter. It's very valuable, he says, but only to members of the Order, which by this point we're capitalising because nobody seems to give it a name, even Ozzie who's writing its history. And, the next thing we know, he's in both Israel and trouble, so Rudy promptly jets off to Tel Aviv to help him out of one or both. He's met by Charlton Heston, a family friend and a professor at Ben Gurion University. Cue that car chase, which is admittedly very effective given the narrow streets involved. Cue Heston's demise.

What's important is that the local authorities believe that Rudy is in Israel not to help his dad but to smuggle artifacts out, so they put him under house arrest ahead of deporting him. And, of course, that's what leads to him abseiling past his guards, disguising himself as a Hasidic Jew and getting into that fantastic sequence, with all its cool fights and stunts and humour.

I did mention humour, right? For two thirds of this picture, the tone is lighthearted, telling a story with tongue at least partway into its cheek. That's rather important, given that Rudy's eventual partner in everything that goes down is Lt. Dalia Barr, one of those Israeli cops who wants him on the next plane out. No, I didn't buy into her sudden realisation at how hinky her orders are and her equally sudden decision to go rogue either, but actress Sofia Milos is decent in the role nonetheless, an early example of those kickass Mossad chicks who would soon become a trope on primetime American TV, which she'd soon join herself as Yelina Salas in *CSI: Miami*.

The biggest mistake the film makes is to completely forget that humour in the third act. Suddenly, we find ourselves watching a serious thriller and the shift in tone is rather jarring, especially given that crucial elements change at the same time.

Most obviously, the Order changes. We've been led to believe that this is some obscure sect of heretics that nobody knows about except Rudy's dad, whose history of them will only be read by fellow academics. Suddenly, there's a heck of a lot of them and they have a really cool temple with pristine stained glass, and they have their hooks into the police and, under the vicious leadership of the new First Disciple Cyrus Jacob, they're ready to blow up Jerusalem and start a holy war.

It's almost as if Scooby and Shaggy had pulled the mask off the villain to uncover not the old lighthouse keeper but, dun dun dah, Osama bin Laden! And, of course, it's up to JCVD and his renegade Israeli cop sidekick to stop him before it's too late. It's hard to tackle this sort of subject matter with humour and the film suffers for ditching it but, frankly, keeping it would have been worse, given that this first reached theatres on 13th December, 2001, only three months after 9/11. No wonder the telegraphed sequel, involving the legendary cities of gold on the Yucatan, didn't happen. Then again, Chuck Norris made that in 1986 and it was worse than this.

- Hal CF Astell

Derailed (2002)

Bruce Willis single-handedly thwarted would-be terrorists in the claustrophobic setting of a besieged office building in *Die Hard* (1988). Then Steven Segal single-handedly thwarted would-be terrorists in the claustrophobic setting of a besieged cruise ship in one of his strongest vehicles, *Under Siege* (1992). In *Derailed* (2002), Jean-Claude Van Damme single-handedly thwarts would-be terrorists in the claustrophobic setting of a besieged passenger train. Sadly, the Belgian action star's entry in the low-rent-*Die Hard*-rip-off-sub-sub-sub-sub-genre is not among his strongest efforts. It is sloppy and uneven and ultimately forgettable.

This time around, Jean-Claude is a secret agent in Europe named Jacques Kristoff. He is talked into doing "one last job" by an unscrupulous superior (Dayton Callie), who has his own self-serving motives. He is ordered to escort Galina (Laura Elena Harring), a high-wire entertainer and master high-tech thief, on a trip by rail. She is secretly in possession of three vials of a deadly toxin - a new generation of smallpox. On top of all this, it just happens to be Kristoff's birthday, and his wife and their two children (who are unaware of his espionage profession) decide to surprise him on the train. They catch him in his cabin with Galina, assume he is being unfaithful, and give him the cold shoulder. So, there is that subplot to deal with. *Simultaneously*, terrorists (led by the impressive Tomas Arana) board the train and hijack it in order to obtain said chemical weapon.

Action ensues. People die. Vials break. Plague spreads. But it all works out in the end. Several characters, including Kristoff's family, are infected by the new plague, but two vials are saved in the finale, which we are told is sufficient to make a vaccine to save them all. However, as Covid 19 has taught us, vaccines are not something that can necessarily be whipped up in time to save those already ailing. So, there is that.

Besides the over-crowded plot - which keeps throwing in new elements rather than developing the ones already established - it is the action scenes which disappoint the most - the very meat and potatoes of the genre. There is action aplenty, don't get me wrong, all of which we've seen before many, many times. It is a steady stream of clichéd set pieces, augmented with poor CG and green-screen effects that scream of artifice.

Despite all that, it is the editing that left me scratching my head the most often. There are many sequences that end with bizarre montages, relying on still images and crude CG, in an attempt, I suppose, at suspenseful style. But instead of accelerating the pace, these digressions cause the momentum – such as it is – to screech to a grinding halt, like a train running into a brick wall. At one point director Bob Misiorowski (who seems unable to control this careening juggernaut) even tries a Brian DePalma-style split screen sequence. We simultaneously see two parallel fight scenes. It's okay for what it is, but it has no resonance with the style (or lack thereof) on display during the rest of the film; and it has none of the complex layering of DePalma's carefully thought-out multiple viewpoints. Somehow in his undistinguished career, Misorowski also managed to produce *Tombstone* (1993), an entertaining re-telling of the gunfight at the OK Corral. It's head and shoulders above the rest of the forgettable titles on his IMDb page.

Most Van Damme movies find some moments to show off his skills on a motorcycle. Scenes which are usually so over the top that all credibility is stretched beyond belief. *Derailed* is no exception. In this one, Jean-Claude rides a commandeered bike over the top of a speeding train, leaping the gaps between the cars at top speed. Then he jumps it off the train, lands on point, and outruns the locomotive. He re-boards the speeding vehicle later on down the line without slowing down, letting the bike tumble into oblivion.

The movie features two literal train wreck scenes, and one metaphorical one, which is the rest of the movie itself (the comparison is irresistible). It is to the movie's credit, however, that some old-school miniature effects are seen sandwiched in between the bad CG effects. The miniature shots are, for the most part, well executed, even if only seen in glimpses. When the miniature train is in flames, however, the technique gives itself away. Still, I am always pleased to see well-executed practical effects in these days of prolific digital fakery.

Of the three stars of low rent action vehicles – the triumvirate of Norris, Segal and Van Damme – JCVD is the one I find most palatable. Norris is always concerned about looking like a squeaky-clean hero of highly moral character. Segal seems only interested in looking like a badass. Van Damme, however, while it is clear his interest is more with the fight scenes than with the human ones, he does seem to *try* to play the scenes as they are written. He may not be the best actor in the game, or even a particularly good one, but he does always seem to me to be giving an honest effort. Sometimes his efforts in *Derailed* hit their mark, and sometimes they do not. But he tries, and *Derailed* is populated with so many day players who seem to have never performed before in their lives, that he comes off okay.

The scenes in which he is most effective are those in which he fears for the life of his son. Some of that honesty may come from the fact that his son in the film is played by his real-life son, Kristopher Van Varenberg. The boy strongly resembles his dad, and even does a mean roundhouse kick or two. Van Varenberg, incidentally, also acquits himself nicely in his performance. The sensitivity on display between the two is probably the most memorable thing about this semi-train wreck of clichés and muddled storytelling.

- Ron Ford

In Hell (2003)

The first thing that stands out about this movie is that wacky font. It puts the *In Hell* in the title as in "What *In Hell* is that supposed to be?" Is this the zany adventures of Johnny Clod and the Van Damme Boys? I'm half-expecting a group of high school nerds trying to get laid over summer break to show up.

But then that title sequence comes and--bam!--wacky font redeemed. There's a fight with a really big dude who looks like Bane and sounds like John Stephenson because I swear, I heard the Great Goblin from the Rankin Bass version of The Hobbit somewhere, but more on him later.

This movie is really told through the eyes of narrator and cellmate 451 (Lawrence Taylor), who dispenses a bit of prison philosophy before—wait--is that the wacky font again? I thought we were past that? We truly are *In Hell*.

It's already difficult for me to take this movie serious. When Kyle LeBlanc (JCVD) finds his wife Grey (Marnie Alton) just murdered, sensitive music plays in the background, tugging ever so gently upon—screw that! Kyle gets hit over the head with a vase by the killer and the Seinfeld bass starts playing. What In Hell? I don't know if I can make it to the end of this.

But here's when the real turnaround happens, not just for the movie, but for me as a viewer. If you've read *Hard to Watch* or *Missing the Action*, specifically my takes in them, you'll know it's fairly irreverent. I dove *In Hell* expecting more of the same: passable acting, bad dialog, near superhuman martial artists, easily identifiable heroes and villains—man does this movie break the mold!

I'm not saying the plot is entirely believable: husband takes revenge on his wife's killer only to end up in a Russian prison fighting in the occasional death match to please the corrupt warden and staff. But where this movie lacks in originality it makes up for in heart. Van Damme's Kyle is *not* badass. In fact, he gets his ass kicked so much you wonder why he accepted the role. And not just by better martial artists, mind you. They're not even. They're all street fighters. And even further he gets his ass handed to him by guards whose only lethal weapons are their clubs and authority.

At first you think he's holding back, waiting for just the right moment to unleash the JCVD beast we all know and love, and you're waiting right along with him. And waiting. And waiting. No. Dude is giving all he's got and still comes up short. But that's the beauty of the movie. He's not top dog who gets away without a scratch. He is three-legged dog hit by a car, begging for scraps.

Of course, he gets better. To a degree. There's no Sensei to lead him in the way. No coach to instruct him. He's on his own. Sure, his cellmate 451 continues with the platitudes, but none of it in itself serves as the catalyst for Kyle's paradigm shift. That comes slowly, incrementally, each time he winds up in the Hole, which is often, and most times, not entirely his fault.

His sole companions in such moments of despair are a butterfly (questionably a hallucination or materialization of his late wife) and the babbling idiot in the hole next to his, who he occasionally tells to shut up by banging on the wall.

The main nemeses are Kravavi Prison guard Tolik (Carlos Gomez) and Russian mafia prisoner Andrei (Raicho Vasilev), the baddest fighter in the prison. Allies include unfortunate prison bitch Billy Cooper (Chris Moir), Coolhand (Billy Rieck), and the questionably motivated Malikai (Alan Davidson).

Eventually Kyle does become top dog, only for 451 to tell us and Kyle that in doing so he has lost himself. With the lesser competition out of the way, prison staff brings out even bigger baddie Valya (Michael Bailey Smith), an import from another prison. Unfortunately for little Billy, he's on the receiving end of Valya's unrestrained passions. Yes, In Hell there are many grave injustices, but in the grand scheme of one hour and 37 minutes, they shall all be dealt great comeuppances.

In the climactic prison fight, where all Hell breaks loose, the prison staff bring out the Bane lookalike/Great Goblin soundalike. I don't know how I didn't see it coming from a mile away, but it chokes me up every time I watch it. It's a beautifully, powerful, touching moment, and another reason this is one of, it not Jean-Claude's most authentic performances.

So, in light of all this, the movie and Jean-Claude Van Damme deserve much respect for their righteous endeavor to stray from the trope-worn path. And for that, I hope Jean-Claude has redeemed himself and doesn't spend the rest of eternity in … *The Expendables.*

- AP Sessler

Las Vegas – "Die Fast, Die Furious" (2004)

This show is centered around the lives of people who run a casino. In this episode, Jean-Claude Van Damme is killed in a stunt accident gone wrong. Of course, this is television, so it can't be an accident, or the episode will go down in history as being ludicrous. There are five seasons of this show, and this is in season one, so it obviously continues. I have never seen an episode of this show before, it feels like another *CSI*, without all the complicated science, though physics played a role in this one.

Jean-Claude has a humorous scene in the beginning where he is being hit on by an attractive blonde and she is as subtle as a jackhammer to the balls. It made me chuckle. There is also a scene where Jean-Claude informs the director of a movie that he (Jean-Claude) will be performing a stunt first. The director is opposed to this behavior. It's funny to note that the director has faith in Jean-Claude's acting but not so much his stunt work. I feel like the opposite is true for every director who has worked with Jean-Claude; however, I could be wrong.

There is the scene of the stunt going wrong, which looked okay for the visual effects required. He is to ride a motorcycle off the top of a building and wave it arms around, however the wire connected to him breaks and he falls to the ground. The motorcycle lands on the camera, thus causing to cut to black (and save time and money to show Jean-Claude dying) it's an effective edit and communicates the idea yet leaves it open to the imagination.

There's also some dry humor in this episode, for example at Jean-Claude's memorial service, instead of using just a headshot, its him holding two guns pointed up. A character remarks that the sequel to *Timecop* is not as good as the first *Timecop*, which is funny for two reasons: 1. Jean-Claude is in the first *Timecop*, but not in the second, and 2. The creator of this show, Gary Scott Thompson, was one of the writers of *Timecop: The Berlin Decision* (the inferior one). I wonder if Thompson is in on that joke or if a writer or an actor got pissed off at him for some reason.

It's hard to rate Jean-Claude's acting because he is playing a version of himself. He plays an actor with the same name and in theory based off characters dialogue, the movies exist in this universe. There is also a funny credit at the end saying that no Jean-Claude's were harmed in the making of this episode. There aren't many Jean-Claude jokes except for the line from the attractive blonde asking if he can still do the splits. The lack of Jean-Claude-based jokes makes it hard to decide if he is in on the humor.

- Stephen Kessen

Narco (2004)

I've had a copy of this film for years, but I've never got round to it until now, not because it's French or because Jean-Claude van Damme has a brief cameo in it as an imagined version of himself, but because I thought it was a drug movie. *Narco*, right? It simply had to be a hagiography of some heroic drug smuggler who hopped over the Mexican border every five minutes back in the 1970s and somehow never got caught? Well, no. Maybe I should have looked beyond its usual title to see that it's also known as *The Secret Adventures of Gustave Klopp*, which hints more appropriately towards what it is, a French dramedy told in the style of ***Amélie and Léolo***. It isn't as good as either of those classics, because it's too long and too convoluted, but it does has plenty to recommend it.

We find out why it's called *Narco* after the opening segment, which is a war scene. Out on the bloody battlefield, a tank rolls up to a solder, just like he's in Tiananmen Square, except that the hatch opens and the driver asks why he doesn't have his four cheese pizza with extra pepperoni. It's called *Narco* because Gustave Klopp is a narcoleptic. He falls asleep at the drop of a hat and dreams about adventures. He's fired from the pizza place, of course, and everywhere else he manages to land a position, but he's not lazy. As he tells us, "I was born with a design flaw."

It's a brutal design flaw, because it most frequently triggers in moments of strong emotion, so he falls asleep as soon as he kisses a girl, even if it's in the middle of a dancefloor. Sex is as problematic as you might expect, but he somehow manages to get Paméla to marry him anyway. At least he makes it through the ceremony, even if he has trouble making it through life. They start to run out of money and the way out is the one that Paméla doesn't want to acknowledge. Gus is a talented artist and he wants to translate his dreams into comic books.

You may be wondering how JCVD is going to get shoehorned into this story and it's all because of Lenny Barr, Gus's best friend. He's a bus driver when we meet him, but only because he had to give up his karate school after beating up a student who had the temerity to badmouth his idol, the one we see in a giant poster on his dojo wall. No guesses for figuring out who that is, of course, because this book is about him.

For the longest time, he's only referenced in dialogue, though it is good dialogue in a film that's full of good dialogue. Lenny talks up *Double Impact* because, if there's anything better than a movie starring JCVD, it's a movie starring two JCVDs. "*Double Impact* was lousy," says the student. "Van Damme sucks." One scene later, Lenny's out of a job.

Eventually van Damme does show up, because Lenny needs a conscience and who better to manifest in that form than his idol? I would explain why, but that way lies spoilers, even though he's not the most reprehensible character here. That's definitely the gentleman who leads Gus's therapy group, a filthy rich wannabe comic book artist who knows a pair of twin ice skating champions turned assassins. What's that? That seems weird to you? You seriously need to watch more French dramedies. They thrive on the quirkiness of their characters and the situation comedy that they wittingly or unwittingly generate. This is far from untypical of the genre.

Of course, you're not here to learn about quirky French dramedies. You're not here to hear about Guy Bennet, a failed comedian turned publisher who owns a schnozzle that recognises talent a mile away. You're certainly not here to imagine the megazoom shot that pulls back from Gus falling asleep in a car park to a giant spaceship shaped like a can of beer. Naturally, that's just so he can portray the hero in the trench scene from *Star Wars*, reimagined just about enough to ensure that Lucasfilm wouldn't file a copyright claim. You're here for JCVD.

Ironically, my better half was also here for JCVD and, I kid you not, she fell asleep before he showed up. In a film about narcolepsy. I'd have to be a scriptwriter for French dramedies to make that up. I did have the courtesy of rewinding, so she could watch that scene. And it's only one scene, that doesn't show up until an hour and a half in and lasts fewer than two minutes. Worse still, our flexible friend from Belgium not only doesn't do the splits but doesn't even stand up. He spends the whole scene sat next to Lenny to convince him that "success without love is nothing".

And he does convince him, in what turns out to be quite the pivotal scene. I may not be fond of the actual ending to this movie but everything up to that point works out exactly as it should and much of that is due to the knock-on effect of JCVD talking to Lenny. He may not be "the greatest of karate men", as his conscience suggests that he is, but he does make the difference in the end, even though he's a sidekick at best and the actor playing him isn't even French. Then again, he's Benoît Poelvoorde, who was glorious in the Belgian mockumentary *Man Bites Dog*, so I ain't judging.

The actual lead, of course, is Gustave Klopp, played by Guillaume Canet, who's most notable for winning a César Award as director of *Tell No One*, even though many might think that dating Marion Cotillard for the past fifteen years trumps that. He's good here, as is Poelvoorde and everyone else, and that includes Jean-Claude van Damme, even if he only gets a skimpy two minutes.

- Hal CF Astell

Wake of Death (2004)

Writing about good movies, especially little-known ones, is fun because I can introduce people to them and what's so good about them. Writing about bad movies can be fun too, if only because it stirs the creative juices. I've written about both in this book and, in every instance, the film I was writing about was, at least, interesting. *Wake of Death* really isn't any of those things. It's another movie and that's about it. I've seen it before, but I'd forgotten everything about it except the decent car stunts at the beginning, which is hardly a great recommendation.

Van Damme is Ben Archer, a former enforcer for organised crime in Marseille who's making a new life for himself as a bouncer in Los Angeles. His wife Cynthia, a social worker for the INS, breaks the rules and brings home a Chinese girl who's been caught up in human trafficking. This triggers the plot because little Kim is the runaway daughter of a Triad boss, Sun Quan, who badly wants her back. It doesn't take long for the body count to start mounting, beginning with the massacre at the Li family restaurant. Cynthia is murdered there and so are her Chinese foster parents, meaning that the legendary Burt Kwouk is gone from the movie just as soon as we realize he's in it. Hey, isn't that... well, it was!

Now Ben Archer is—and you can start reading in deep movie trailer voice—out for vengeance in the *Wake of Death*!

I could focus on the good bits, to persuade you into watching.

Van Damme is brutal in this one, always giving the impression that he's not holding back and for good reason. He's never been the greatest actor in the world, but he has a good attempt at grief here and there are at least a couple of scenes where he sells it well. There are some great shots too. Before Archer takes down Andy Wang in a brothel, he shoots someone through the legs of a hooker as she runs downstairs. He throws a bad guy down the hole in a winding spiral staircase. There's even a fantastic shot of an old woman simply counting money; Archer walks past in a ski mask and she merely smiles, because she knows exactly what comes next.

Or I could focus on the bad bits, to persuade you that there are much better movies out there.

The script isn't as clear as my synopsis makes it seem. We have to figure out relationships for ourselves, even names, because the film doesn't really care about telling us. For instance, I don't think Cynthia is ever called anything except "my wife" and only Van Damme speaks the word "Nicholas", so we think he's really called Nicola. There are important supporting characters of note, like wheelchair bound Max and his French gangsters, but we have to go to Wikipedia to figure out how they connect. And there's Tony, who does quite a lot, though it utterly failed to register on me whether he was a cop or a brother or a friend. I'm still not sure I've figured that out yet.

Maybe the reason why there are so many good bits and so many bad bits, not to forget the far more numerous merely OK bits, is that *Wake of Death* was a fragmented production.

It started out with Ringo Lam as the director, who knows the heroic bloodshed genre well, which is what this film seems like it maybe kinda sorta wants to be. He made *Full Contact*, starring Chow Yun Fat and Simon Yam—the latter of whom is the big bad here, Sun Quan—and, of course, he made both *Replicant* and *In Hell* with Van Damme, both of which are far more recommended than *Wake of Death*. However, he left the film soon into shooting in Canada.

Cess Silvera took over for a couple of weeks in South Africa before Philippe Martínez finished the job, even though each had only racked up a single directorial credit before this. There were four writers, two cinematographers, even two editors. No wonder it seems to be a hundred things all at the same time but never truly any of them.

I should have cared about all sorts of things here, but I didn't. Did I mention that this is all about heroin? Never mind; it doesn't matter. I almost cared about the corruption but only because the plot conveniences generated by who's corrupt are annoyingly obvious. I especially should have cared about the kids, both Kim and Nicola, but they didn't seem to matter. We have no doubt that Ben Archer is going to save Kim, because the film would be pointless otherwise, but we have no idea if he'll be able to save Nicola too and we really don't care. Sorry, kiddo!

Instead, I ended up caring about little details that shouldn't matter in the slightest. Where can I buy one of those bathtubs that the Archers have that's large enough to house two people very comfortably indeed? When Van Damme's long grieving scene ends with a man leaping through his window with a sword, is that a nod to Burt Kwouk's work as Cato in the *Pink Panther* movies, given that he was in this film too for about a minute? Why is the motorcycle chase in an empty mall so cool when it's also so gratuitous? Most of all, why doesn't the truck driver in the stunt scene that opens the movie just stop? That fundamental question is probably why I remembered that section and forgot everything else.

So, *Wake of Death* exists. It's a JCVD movie and he actually acts in it. There are explosions and fire stunts and gunplay. There's Simon Yam, who doesn't know how to not to do the business. There's a French gangster in a wheelchair. It's good when it's good, it's bad when it's bad and the rest of it is just there.

- Hal CF Astell

Second in Command (2006)

I try not to let political opinions influence my reviews. I want the film to stand on its own merits, however the subject matter of Second in Command feels like someone ripped the headlines off a newspaper in December of 2020, went back into 2005, wrote a screenplay, decided to set it in a second or third world country, and film it. I am writing this as the United States of America finishes up an election where Joe Biden won with 81 million votes and 306 electoral college votes, solidifying him to be the next President of the United States. Donald Trump has yet to concede and has filed lawsuits trying to get states to overturn their election results. I am writing this on December 29, 2020. Biden has yet to be sworn in and Trump has not admitted defeat, some are concerned for military action being used to influence (reject and disregard) election results. Many fear some similar actions being taken in 2020, like those that are depicted in this film.

It starts off when Sam Keenan (Jean-Claude Van Damme) is assigned to security at the U.S. Embassy in Moldavia. He sees the civil war that is taking place in the country during the time of this controversial election. The president-elect eventually makes his way to the embassy and brings trouble with him unintentionally.

Simon Fellows directs this movie with a style of simplicity, which isn't bad, just not as interesting to watch. Actors move, talk, and the performances are fine. No noteworthy camera moves or anything. It's a shame given the subject matter that one could feel bored when watching this film, but it was boring to me. I was uninterested in the president or if anyone killed him. I will forever wonder what drew Fellows to this frequently boring story.

The cinematography is mostly hand-held which creates a sense of a documentary feel to it, which given the subject matter is one of the better creative decisions this film makes. I would have color corrected it differently, a good portion of the film has an almost sepia tone to it, which is not fun to look at when it's done for a while. It also clashes with the higher contrasted footage used in the film as well. That's more of an editor choice I know, when it comes to cinematography, it was well done. Douglas Milsome helms the cameras here as the cinematographer and has had a varied career. He worked on big films like *Full Metal Jacket* and *Robin Hood: Prince of Thieves*. He knows what he is doing, I just can't get over the sepia tone.

The writing of the film gets the job done. It's not a film you have to think too much about. It has a certain number of lines you expect "Get down," "You're my second in command," etc. It's not laughable, but don't look for creative dialogue or a too interesting of a plot. After a while, these films just become about the body count and how creative the kills be. With this film, most of the people are shot, which doesn't make it interesting. There is an exploding bus sequence that made me go, "well at least they are trying."

The acting is fine; Jean-Claude takes charge as his character does. Some actors know what lines they need to milk, like when Keenan is told, "You're my second in command." the camera zooms in on that actor's face like he just issued a decree, or at least was desperate to make the trailer for the film. A majority of the action requires emotive content ranging from being either angry, concerned, or indifferent. I was particularly drawn to a character who seemed to always have his camera out. I keep going back to the adage, "The revolution will be televised." this character seemed to embody that, and you got a sense of the goal of the character. I think we all have a goal of recording something historically significant or culturally influential and it's nice to see that character depicted on screen in a move where a character like that would be too intelligent for screenwriter to introduce.

When it comes to Jean-Claude Van Damme as Keenan, he does the role justice. We are treated to a scene near the end where Van Damme shows off his martial art skills as well as some fun knife play. It doesn't warrant a recommendation to watch this movie as it was quite boring, overall, which is sad given the unfortunate timing of when I watched it. I wanted to recommend this movie, but when I look at the subject matter, is there a film that deals with similar things a lot better and to be honest, I enjoyed the *13 Hours* film directed by Michael Bay about the Benghazi attacks more than I enjoyed this film and I barely enjoyed that film. I also enjoyed *Zero Dark Thirty*, a film about the hunt for Bin Laden. This film felt more about the bureaucracy of dealing with the attack on the embassy over the attack on the embassy itself.

I wanted to like this film. I like films that feel like they could be talking about the world in which we are living and offering a viewpoint. I think I expected too much out of this film as I was bored when watching it. I normally track how many times I look at my watch on a movie, but I didn't need to this time, I real timed reviewed this movie, pausing the movie at interesting or noteworthy parts and thankfully that comes along with a status bar showing the run time and how much is left. I am not saying that I would rather watch the timeline than this movie, but it was constantly at the bottom of my video streamer.

- Stephen Kessen

The Hard Corps (2006)

This movie had me dreading the remainder within the first few minutes just because of how they did the title credits. It plays over slow motion, which is cool given the subject matter, however the font is bright white and filled in, when we see the title card for *The Hard Corps*, it's a thin transparent outline, which is inconsistent with other credits, I know it sounds insignificant, but it drove me insane. Someone made the decision to change it just for the title. If you want to emphasis it, just make it bigger, hall make it a different color, but to do the complete opposite, is jarring.

The movie starts off when a rap mogul gets out of prison on parole, which leads to discomfort for Tamara Barclay (Vivica A Fox). The scene quickly gives out exposition in a nice three course meal where you don't have to go hunting for it. The team quickly decides that they need extra security. Tamara and her brother Wayne run a real estate company and they are afraid the rap mogul Terrell (Viv Leacock) will put a hit out on them since he has a reputation for putting hits out on the competition. Terrell gives a shit about his probation for about ten seconds before he tries to assemble a team.

Tamara hires the extra security in the form of Philip (Jean-Claude Van Damme) a former solider rattled with PTSD he suffered from Afghanistan and Iraq. This is a good role for Van Damme, he plays the tortured soul well, better than most actors, as I mentioned in my review of *We Die Young*.

Sheldon Lettich directs his film with more care than most direct to video films. He started his career with Van Damme directing *Lionheart* back in 1990 and *Double Impact* a year later. He lets the actors act and move naturally. The camera angles make sense. It's a testament to style where he storyboards a film, shoots it, doesn't try to get too creative which inconsequential matters, and then creates a film that is actually worth watching. He is one of the few to go from theatrical releases to direct to video fare, and then go back to theaters as he did in 2015 with a family movie called *Max* (Boaz Yakin directed the film with a script co-written with Lettich).

The writing of this film belongs to both Lettich and George Saunders (who also has close to 40 writing credits to his name). The dialogue isn't bad, but I didn't find any quotable lines in it. There's nothing to make fun of here, but there is nothing to point out to recommend, except for an amusing segment where they want the extra security to blend in, and Philip sticks out like a sore thumb. It was good for a chuckle. This is the type of movie where you can compare it to other direct to video fare and realize the different between good writing and bad writing. I feel that there is an unwritten or unspoken law that says direct to video means lower quality, which is untrue. It does fall into a cliche of the era where the use of hip hop music dominates the soundtrack. I don't know how I feel about a rapper being the main villain of the movie, but it's better than a drug lord, more original than someone who killed so in so's brother, wife, child… you know what I mean. I have seen worse movies in theaters, and I have seen better movies that went direct to video.

Acting wise, this film has some good performances. Van Damme gets his paycheck and Fox brings some humanity to a part usually reserved for a more supporting character. She never feels like a hostage or a damsel in distress, but more of a tag along. She gives out the exposition and explains why the extra security would be needed. A worse script would have killed that character off as they served their purpose. Sadly, she also gets used as a romantic interest for Phillip, which I have seen way too many times, but it's played with dignity.

Okay, so let's get to some Van Damme. As I stated earlier, this role is great for him. He is great at playing soldiers with trauma. He's not afraid to get emotional and show vulnerability, given the subject matter. It's not an Oscar winning role by any means, but it's a good fit for him. You also get to see some awesome Van Damme kicks and one even causes a man to go out of a window. It's a gritty scene that is well shot. There is more gunplay in this film as opposed to his use of martial arts, which is a downside, but it still has the action that audiences want. One fight scene takes place in a boxing gym, but not in the ring, it takes place beside the ring because, why not? I enjoyed the scene even though it did seem weird to direct it that way.

It's hard for me to say if I would recommend it or not, it did its job, I wasn't bored, but I wasn't rushing to tell all my friends to see it. If you like Jean-Claude Van Damme and have the five dollars to kill, sure see it. I am glad it was five dollars though, if I paid like ten or fifteen dollars a ticket plus the cost of snacks at the theatre, I probably would have been a little pissed off at my financial stupidity. The eye candy of women in bikinis was a nice touch, but I feel like it's been done far too many times to have it feel fresh. The soundtrack doesn't have an "it" song, just whatever rap songs they could find. Jean-Claude's good performance barely elevates a painfully average movie.

- Stephen Kessen

Heist School (2006)

In 2004, American's saw a teen comedy called *The Perfect Score*, which deals with a group of students trying to steal the S.A.T. answers, which on its own, several sources have claimed that is "impossible." In 2006, the country of Turkey took the similar concept, threw more complex filmmaking techniques on it, and released it on the world. I would love to say the editor probably did a line of cocaine and went, "you know what, this scene should have a green hue to it," and then just did it. It doesn't adhere to normal looking films. This director wanted to create a visually interesting film about an important social situation and provide commentary on the world we live in and the importance of education. The director succeeded with flying colors with that endeavor.

The opening scenes features a sequence that feels like a dream where a student is in a police interrogation; it looks like a police interrogation from the outside, you got the good cop and the bad cop, however instead of asking questions like, "Who did it?" or, "Where were you last night?" it deals with them trying to find X in a math problem. It's an analogy I felt in my soul and with the importance put on that end of the year tests in school. I know several high school students and maybe even some college students who will feel the same way.

The premise is the same, the kids try to steal the quiz answers and get into good schools. It's the filmmaking techniques that make it rise above the 2004 American version. This version is not afraid to get a little darker with the lives of the students. One student finds out that his mother has cancer. It helps you feel for the character. There is also a motif of a horse race and trying-to-win-to—come-out-on-top feel. It's an interesting analogy, because when I think of a horse race, I think of finishing first, which doesn't make sense in relation to the exams. It's a visual the filmmakers held on for the duration.

The direction of the film is simple, camera angles make sense, the kids walk and talk. Nothing stands out in terms of the direction, but that's not a bad thing. The camera angles are fun and can sometimes be visually interesting. It does a really good job in scenes of interrogation where you feel like all the eyes are on you.

The most fascinating aspect of the film is the editing, sometimes the scenes are long tracking shots, which are more complicated than what we, as the audience, give them credit for. Other times, it's cut cut cut in rapid succession and, given the theme of the heist, it makes sense.

Some scenes are shown in normal coloring, others have a greenish hue to them, others are black and white, some a sepia; it creates an interesting visual. I usually have a hard time with foreign films (the whole movie is done in Turkish) but the visual kept me focused on the film and it makes one wonder how the medium of film is created and represented in different countries. The main question from this, culturally, is did American filmmaking have a strong influence on world cinema, or did we steal ideas from other countries. Regardless, *Heist School* has an American vibe in some scenes, especially when they discuss the, well, heist.

The acting in the film is surprisingly effective, the actors look like they care about the parts they are playing. Nothing screams Academy Award or Razzie. Jean-Claude seems to enjoy making fun of his bad-ass persona in this film. He emerges from an airplane wearing sunglasses and a jacket that just flows in the wind. He is the one the students ask to get the answers to the test. Jean seems to know that the scene works best when played as straight as possible, because that is exactly how he plays it.

Jean-Claude has the smoothest performance within this movie, because he plays Charles, which is not his real name. Charles' real name is Jean-Claude Van Damme and he was hired by a

former student to pretend to give the answers to the test. It ends on a familiar theme in that cheaters never win. It was a weird twist in the movie especially since one of the kids acknowledges that he looks like

Jean-Claude Van Damme. What is most unusual is that Jean-Claude speaks English in the movie and the students seem to understand, which is weird because English isn't even listed as a minority language. The language of Turkey is Turkish (imagine that) but there is also Kurdish and about 1% of the population speaks Arabic. I wonder if his language was dubbed for the film, but it looks like and sounds like Jean-Claude Van Damme. This movie is a tough sell from a marketing standpoint. It's a Turkish film where they switch between Turkish, English, and French (I have never been so happy for subtitles).

I enjoyed the film, but it's a trippy experience with the editing and visualizations that the director incorporated. I didn't laugh enough for me to consider it a comedy and I think with the themes of death of a parent and wanting a better life, it wouldn't work as a light-hearted comedy. It really makes you feel like it's the end of the world if the students don't do well on this exam. The social commentary hits hard and it left me thinking about it afterwards. I always thought with other countries making it easier for kids to afford college, they still have to go through the trouble of accepting you. It's not enough just to afford going to college, the college has to want you and the college wants those test scores. If this film was an exam, I would give the director a B+. It's worth a study.

- Stephen Kessen

Until Death (2007)

This is a tough entry into Jean-Claude van Damme's filmography and rarely in a good way. It's a New Orleans film that fails to make use of its location, somehow appearing to be set in a generic city. It's a nemesis movie, a long and drawn-out slog between cop and criminal, but the latter hardly even shows up, Stephen Rea reliably good but somewhat inconsequential, because he's a MacGuffin rather than a character. It's an epic shootout picture, with a pivotal scene in which every plot strand comes together at once in the inevitable abandoned warehouse, but I found that I really didn't care. In fact, if I ever came to care, I'd have a choice of endings, as the European and U.S. versions of the film differ as to whether JCVD's character lives or dies.

So, with absolutely nothing to play for, I'll explain what I liked about this movie and what I liked most is that I didn't like JCVD, at least for half of the movie. His colleagues call him Tony Stowe, experienced narcotics detective on the New Orleans force. His wife Valerie calls him Anthony, though she'd rather not call him at all. I didn't get a name for his sideburns, which are a character all of their own, enough so that it would be possible to conjure up a fan theory that they're the supernatural source of all his troubles.

And he has serious troubles, because he's a complete and utter bastard in this movie, who isn't liked by anyone—not his colleagues, not his wife, not even his former partner, Gabriel Callahan, who's now a crime lord on the ascendant. And not us, which makes this portrayal rather refreshing, and I'm happy to let you know that JCVD sells it surprisingly well, almost like James McAvoy playing Bruce Springsteen, if, of course, Bruce Springsteen was a complete and utter bastard of a dirty New Orleans cop. Let me give you some highlights.

When a cop's fiancée gets killed during a failed sting Stowe put together, his idea of sympathy is throwing him to the station floor. When another cop calls in a favour from him, to help his pot-dealing son avoid jail time, he turns him in. When his wife wants to meet him at a karaoke bar, he rapes a hooker on a pool table first ("I won't charge you if you won't charge me"). When Valerie tells him that she's pregnant by another man, he rages outside and beats up the men trying to tow his car, before driving away to shoot up with heroin.

What works here is that van Damme is very believable as Tony Stowe. He's not Bad Lieutenant. He's not an outright villain. He may even believe, if he doesn't think about it too deeply, that he's still a good cop. However, he's so far out over the edge that nobody in his life would agree with that assessment, and there's no easy way back. Even if he could succeed in taking down Callaghan, which success has eluded him for a decade now, he's more likely to just fall apart completely than come clean. That quest is arguably the only thing keeping him remotely stable. Without it, he's nothing.

And, when Callaghan shoots him in the head at close range halfway through the movie in what is the definition of a pivotal scene, it's arguably that quest and only that quest that provides him with enough will to live. He's in a coma, naturally, from the massive shock of the event, but the bullet came in under his chin, bounced off his jaw and missed everything vital.

A regular viewer might interpret a coma as the best thing for his ravaged body, because the nurses do not have a heroin drip handy and so only feed the appropriate drugs into his system so that he can heal. A regular viewer might understand how this inadvertent cold turkey might sweep away the drug-addled haze that he's been under for years and allow him to start afresh. A regular viewer might believe that the inevitably slow recovery from such a traumatic event would give a survivor a whole new perspective on life, as a perfect opportunity to rethink what truly matters.

And maybe that's what the writers Dan Harris and James Portolese intended, perhaps aiming this dark and gritty dirty cop action thriller at the Lifetime Channel, but I'm not a regular viewer. I have decades of horror movies behind me. I'm going to focus in on a tiny detail that regular viewers would miss and blow it up out of all proportion. Clearly to me, the routine shaving of the Sideburns of Evil by nurses working valiantly to save a man's life released Tony Stowe from whatever curse he happened to be under and let him be himself again. Screw Lifetime. I choose to believe Harris and Portolese were aiming at Shudder, even if it didn't launch for eight years after this movie's release. Details, details.

Whatever the reason, the tone of this movie shifts on a dime. Callaghan is still carving a bloody swathe through his opposition, but it's in the newspaper headlines. Stowe recovers, physically and emotionally, working not only to repair his body but also some of the damage that he had wrought on so many people over so much time. And you can write the rest of the script from there, maybe for the Lifetime Channel and maybe for Shudder, depending on your outlook.

To my thinking, the film is an emotional zoom into the heart of darkness for half its running time, perhaps trying to see how far an audience might be willing to allow the filmmakers to take van Damme in that direction, and then an emotional pull back during the other half, perhaps trying to see if they could still redeem his character given how far he'd gone over the edge. Does it work even a little bit? Watch the movie.

- Hal CF Astell

The Shepard (2008)

In Kabul, American soldiers sure know how to overuse complex wrestling moves when attempting to sneak into places. They're looking for someone called Jamal al-Adin but they find a woman with a bomb strapped to her chest instead. Amazingly enough, she doesn't talk when they threaten to blow her up. Yeah, she does that herself. Who'd a thunk it? Clearly, these aren't going to be our good guys. Fortunately, they get brighter by the time they become our bad guys.

Two years later, in the film's present, Jean-Claude Van Damme arrives in Columbus, NM with his pet rabbit strapped into his passenger seat. Both are called Jack. The one we assume we should be paying attention to is Jack Robideaux, a former New Orleans homicide cop who's in town to join the Border Patrol. Why, we'll find out later, even though we really want to know why he takes his rabbit to the local bar.

Robideaux joins the Border Patrol in time to discover that there's a new breed of smuggler operating in the region. They're well-funded, they're well trained, they're well-armed and they're, well, former U.S. military. They all served with one man, who we soon discover is Benjamin Meyers, supposedly killed in action but really alive and well and orchestrating a major smuggling operation from his base in Mexico. He's played by Stephen Lord, who was also in *Until Death* the previous year, but Scott Adkins is one of his henchmen, so we know which fight we're waiting for.

It won't surprise you to find that Robideaux makes a difference immediately: saving his new partner, Billy Pawnell, from being shot in the office; stopping a mugging in town that splashes him across the news, courtesy of a local politico seeking re-election; and realizing that a shooting match across the border fence is just a diversion. He figures out what it's a diversion from too, so Jack and Billy are able to stop an incursion a little further away. He even manages to catch one of the migrants before they all make it back across the border, but it turns out to be the one who's strapped with C4.

I don't think it's a spoiler, by the way, to point out that the bomb squad don't manage to save him. Hey, every action movie needs explosions! Meyers is clearly a great villain because he knows what action movies need and he continually delivers it, however ridiculous it would be in real life. I'm guessing that, while international drug smugglers may well have cool swimming pools for topless women to frolic around in, they probably don't electrify them and hang their enemies upside down above them for questioning. That smacks of the sort of shenanigans we get from James Bond villains.

Beyond what's important to include in an action movie, we learn a lot here. We learn that 2008 was surprisingly a crappy year for computer graphics. We learn that 743.94.056.329 is apparently a valid IP address. We learn that picking a fight in a bar with a man trying to quietly eat a cheeseburger with his pet rabbit is a terrible idea.

The stupidest lesson we learn is that apparently nobody cares about border issues in an election year. Yeah, that made me double take too! This was made only eight years before the Age of Trump, but it feels like a different century. The most believable lesson is that there are only two reasons to join the Border Patrol: to uphold the law and to beat up Mexicans.

Naturally, Robideaux has a third reason. He does uphold the law, but only when it suits him. He also beats up Mexicans, but only the bad ones and not because they're Mexicans; he beats up Americans too, when the urge takes him. But neither drives him and to understand what does, we need to learn more about Jack the rabbit. You knew he wasn't here to savage knights of the round table.

The film takes place in both Mexicos, New and old, but it was shot in Bulgaria, which doesn't quite work but is no worse than when Hollywood usually pretends something is something else. So, these are Bulgarians playing Mexicans? Shrug. It's no less valid than having Native Americans play Mexicans and vice versa and Hollywood's been doing that for a century and more.

What we really don't buy is the fact that, even after the film shows us a border crossing manned by armed guards, it allows anyone and his dog to get through. The bad guys just have to dress up as priests. The good guys just have to not use their brakes. Can you imagine the international incident that would arise if armed Federales drove into El Paso, Nogales or Calexico and killed a bunch of bad guys? Well, apparently that doesn't apply to JCVD doing the same thing in Puerto Palomas, Chihuahua.

It's sloppy writing to not find a more believable way for Robideaux to end up at Meyers's compound. I won't call the twists sloppy, but I will say that they aren't remotely surprising. Frankly, at this point, we're only still watching because we want to see the inevitable Van Damme vs. Adkins fight scene and find out what's up with Jack the rabbit. The latter turns out to be disappointing, but the former is decent. Sure, Van Damme is padded up like the Michelin Man, so we wonder if Adkins can't pull his kicks, but there's a reason for this within the story, so it's OK. With a quick mention for Natalie J. Robb who does a good job as Robideaux's new boss, Capt. Ramona Garcia, in a picture where acting really isn't anyone's top priority, I'll end with Van Damme's sense of humor, which I'm realizing from his later movies and short films like JCVD's "Day Out" is very cool indeed. Then again, it kind of has to be when you knowingly sign up to be upstaged by a rabbit.

- Hal CF Astell

JCVD (2008)

Let's just be honest here right out of the gate. Jean-Claude Van Damme is many things, but a comedy savant he is (probably) not. Legend has it that writers purposely bungled lines to give him funny dialogue on his (surprisingly) effective turn in an episode of "Friends" (covered elsewhere in more, er, *detail* in this very book).

That said, *JCVD* finds him in one of his most impressive and witty parts, with his early action scenes and reactions serving as pretty damn subtly funny punchlines. And even though it was going to be hard to dislike an action film with lines like, "Chuck Norris works for the CIA", and the recurring "Van Damme left this shithole to head to Hollywood", Van Damme takes the likability level to a new, unheralded level. He's never been this empathetic AND likable in the same film, to my recollection, and *JCVD* is pretty easily one of his best offerings overall, if not his *best*.

"Jean-Claude Van Damme's robbing a post office. Possible hostage situation."

JCVD manages the tricky feat of using Van Damme's past movies and history to build the character of himself, and aside from being a pretty comical and dynamic narrative, there is also some not-so-subtle commentary on the public's adoration of celebrity and the hero worship of icons. In this case, it transcends even the notion of what appears to be a violent crime, with Van Damme greeted by a throng of fans cheering him on outside the bank where they believe he is holding hostages and stealing stuff.

In reality, our hero has just walked into a situation and immediately become a key player in a crime that he has no real part in. Presumably, once he is recognized by the REAL (somewhat inept) post office robbers, they evolve whatever their previous plan is to include Van Damme as their faux ringleader.

The subplot finds JCVD embroiled in a custody situation, with effectively sobering scenes lending more empathy to his character, as well as a second subplot that has him yearning to be in a major studio movie even at the detriment of his own personal monetary take. In short, he wants to make a "real" movie, and he cares more about the fact that he has lost his daughter in custody than anything concerning his career.

The irony, of course, is that this movie IS a "real" movie. In fact, *JCVD* is a truly good movie, bordering on great. After the initial plot with the post office unfolds, we're given a pretty genius look at the same situation from Van Damme's point of view. Van Damme has stumbled into something here…a script that allows him to show some actual acting chops. He's allowed to show a number of emotions and to his credit, he does this all quite well, veering from amusement, to frustration, to anger…even joy. And best of all may be this new (at least to us) mastery of the deadpan delivery, and even more surprisingly, out and out *vulnerability*. Who knew?

Maybe Van Damme knew; maybe he was stuck hiding this performance behind a multitude of 'B' movies, ranging from watchable to…let's just say *not so watchable*. Truth be told, not many of his screenplays have ever given him much to work with. That said, it's pretty safe to say that Van Damme at age 25 would not be capable of giving such a performance. It is partially built upon our prior knowledge of his career and reputation as an action actor, sure, but beyond that, it's tough to see a youthful Van Damme dropping his guard long enough to send himself – and his genre – up in such a manner.

There is a riotous scene in which he and one of his captors debate the merits of John Woo films, and Van Damme tells the guy, "At least he made *Face Off*," which is met with something along the lines of, "Yeah, but he could have used YOU for that…. still, at least you avoided *Windtalkers*."

This leads into another funny exchange in which the bad guy is grilling him about future projects, specifically one that he has read about on the internet. Van Damme humbly (and sadly) informs him that he has lost that part to Steven Seagal. Van Damme (hilariously) thinks the reason they chose Steve is because he cut off his ponytail. The fella isn't buying it. After all, "You're TEN TIMES better than Steven Seagal", he says, and anyone watching *JCVD* with any semblance of objectivity would be hard pressed to disagree.

What becomes apparent to viewers of JCVD is that this movie is at least partially so successful because Van Damme trusts the writers and the filmmakers. He treats every line like its legitimate and doesn't wink at the camera. We never get the feeling that he feels like the material is beneath him. He plays scenes where he is basically being treated like a performing monkey the way an exhausted, exasperated, well known icon *would*. That's paramount to the success of *JCVD*; anything less, anything more 'tongue-in-cheek", any feeling that Van Damme doesn't truly *understand* the material, and the flick could still be fun…but not the great vehicle that it is.

In short, Jean-Claude has done more than just stumble into a really good movie; he is a huge reason WHY the movie is really good. *JCVD* is a testament to the power of celebrity, yes, but it's also a look into the actual talent that JCVD (the man) possesses, aside from the uncanny ability to sidekick a cigarette out of a nervous man's mouth.

- Paul Counelis

Robot Chicken – "Maurice Was Caught" (2009)

I had never seen an episode of *Robot Chicken* when I took on this assignment and from this 11-minute episode, I can tell you, I am looking forward to new episodes. This episode contains animated/Claymation style skits that usually end in violence or with a sick twist.

The first skit contains a man going to fight Dracula at his castle where Jean-Claude Van Damme plays Dracula. The joke of this episode is that the man fights with a whip, which makes all his enemies laugh, until they are hit with it and then they complain about the pain they are in. I laugh way too hard at the line, "I can't feel my fingers." The man quickly reaches Dracula where the vampire taunts the man telling him that his father died in that spot. The man then whips our undead friend and Dracula complains about the pain before muttering, "I don't have to stand for this," and turns into a bat. The man then whips the now-bat version of Dracula as people look on and try to figure out if it is a sexual fetish.

The second skit was so short the paragraph I am typing will take longer to read than the skit lasted. It features a judge who tries to throw the book (literally) at a man in court, but it doesn't make it. The bailiff then gets the book, the judge thanks him, and then successfully hits the defendant.

One skit involves a nerd character accidentally hacking into the government computer system when he thought it was playing a computer game. He ends up launching a missile which then causes the S.W.A.T. team to bust down his down and demand to tell him that the location he was looking for (Mordor of all places) is in Afghanistan. Jean-Claude has no part in this skit.

Jean also voices the Rhett Butler character in a remade version of *Gone With The Wind* called *Frankly, My Dear, I Don't Give a Van Damme* (get it) where it reimagines the Civil War classic as a kung fu film (one I would kill to see in real life).

The rest are R rated twists on popular media like a *Sesame Street* parody where one of the Muppets just complains about economics. Then there was also one of Little Orphan Annie in an almost *Clueless*-like parody. It got a little too weird but the scenes that had Jean-Claude in it were great for his casting. I hope he does play Dracula in a real-life film; his voice works so well for it.

I want to see what other comedy *Robot Chicken* has to offer. It's like taking a *Saturday Night Live* episode and making it 10 minutes long. It gives you barely enough time to grasp the concept, get the joke, laugh, and then you are off to the next skit. My head!

- Stephen Kessen

Universal Soldier: Regeneration (2009)

Yeah, here's another *Universal Soldier* movie and it's the second, third, fourth or fifth in the series, depending on how you count. It came out in 2009, so it's the fifth movie to be released, but it the second with Dolph Lundgren in the cast and the third with Jean-Claude Van Damme. It's also the third to make it into cinemas but it's written as a direct sequel to the original, completely ignoring the prior direct sequel to the original, *Universal Soldier: The Return*, and the two made for cable sequels, *Universal Soldier II: Brothers in Arms* and *Universal Soldier III: Unfinished Business*, somehow making this the fourth second film in the series. Are you with me so far?

What that ridiculously convoluted paragraph means is that you can ignore most of what you've read thus far about the *Universal Soldier* movies in this book. All you need to remember is that Luc Deveraux and Andrew Scott were sent to Vietnam where they killed each other in 1969. Van Damme played the former and he was a good guy. Lundgren played the latter, and he wasn't, at least when we meet him, because he's gone batshit crazy, killed everyone else under his command and made a necklace out of their ears. Their bodies are promptly packed in ice and shipped back to Nevada where they're reanimated by a vastly funded and completely illegal military program as super soldiers with superpowers who will never say no to their bosses. Except, of course, when they do because that's why we have a movie. And three direct sequels. And two sequels to two different direct sequels.

That movie ended with Deveraux alive and Scott very dead, given that his last moments involved being fed through a combine harvester and spat out in very tiny gobbets of flesh. As final scenes go, that one was pretty final. However, given that both these actors are back here, the first challenge for the scriptwriter is to conjure something up to make us believe how and, quite frankly, Victor Ostrovsky doesn't even bother. Instead, he hits us so hard and so fast with gritty action that we almost forget about it. It's only when Van Damme and Lundgren show back up that we start thinking about thinking about it again.

What happens is that a terrorist organization kidnaps the kids of the Ukrainian prime minister, spirits them off to Chernobyl and threatens to kill them by blowing up the still functioning reactor #3, with them inside, if their demands are not met. The man in charge is Commander Topov and the NGU, or Next-Generation UniSol (Universal Soldier), who took the kids, is played by Andrei "The Pit Bull" Arlovski, a former UFC heavyweight champion. Realising this, the good guys send in not only a platoon of American soldiers to retrieve the hostages but four original generation UniSols as well, who were specially thawed out for the occasion. The NGU doesn't care, of course. Only two regular soldiers make it out alive. This is a sequel. Everything has to be bigger and better.

So where are our stars? Well, Van Damme has been recuperating in Switzerland. From what, we're not told. Is he Luc Devereaux from the first Universal Soldier, merely a decade and a half older than he ended that film? Or is he an alternate Luc Devereaux, the same first generation UniSol but with a different history? Why are we trying to reintegrate him back into society? No answers are forthcoming, because the script doesn't care for background. Certainly, anyone starting the series here would be able to follow it without any trouble, in fact probably better than anyone who had seen any of the previous films, including the first one.

Oddly, the plot we've been given is mostly ended before Devereaux enters the fray. Sure, he's brought back in and upgraded, but he hasn't faced a single bad guy by the time the Ukrainian prime minister gives in and Topov switches off the bomb. It all ought to end there, but Dr. Robert Colin, the rebel American scientist hired to bring in the NGU, had bad skin and was bullied as a kid so he won't give up the power he suddenly has. Enter Andrew Scott, whose cryochamber he conveniently had on hand just because.

And Scott is immediately troubled, once again with no reason given. Given where we end up, we can only assume that he isn't the result of stitching those gobbets of flesh together but of cloning the original soldier and ending up with something big and tough but almost endearingly broken. He's much more sympathetic than last time. Of course, Colin is so blissfully stupid that he actually tells Dolph Lundgren to sit, like he's a giant puppy. Scott crushes his skull and that's it for his plans for world domination. Oh dear, what a pity, never mind.

What follows is a heck of a lot of action compressed into a surprisingly small amount of time. Once all the faceless terrorist extras are taken care of, we're set for a redux of Van Damme vs. Lundgren, merely with Arlovski stuck in the middle wondering what to do now that his plot is apparently over, and another soldier, Capt. Kevin Burke, who may or may not be a UniSol, sent into the fray for good measure.

Everything gets resolved, kinda, sorta, except for all the questions we came in with, which is an odd approach for a script to take. Instead, we're left wondering about what this sequel is actually a sequel to. Is this third direct sequel to an old film really a direct sequel to that old film or is it a reimagination of it? It's kind of the latter, but without any of the background a reimagination needs because it thinks it's a sequel. It's enough to make you break out in hives. And get picked on. Then plan to take over the world by telling Dolph Lundgren to sit.

- Hal CF Astell

Kung Fu Panda 2 (2011)

Picking up after the events of *Kung Fu Panda*, Po Ping has been the Dragon Warrior for about a year now and has a decent handle on his ever-increasing Kung Fu abilities. That's when an evil peacock decides to attempt to take over all of China using a new weapon that will wipe out the need for Kung-Fu. At the very end of the movie, Po's biological father made a cameo where in a single line he realized his son was still alive. The film was directed by Jennifer Yuh Nelson and starts Jack Black, Angelina Jolie, Dustin Hoffman, Gary Oldman, Jacki Chan, Seth Rogen and more A-list celebrities returning for the sequel.

The movie is a solid sequel, I had to watch the first in order to make sure I knew what was going on, though it turns out it wasn't necessary to understand this movie. Other than Po being the Dragon Warrior and how he got to that title, nothing from the first movie is really needed for this movie. Po and the Furious Five, Tigress, Crane, Monkey, Mantis and Viper, travel to a city far away from their home to take on Peacock after he took over that city and imprisoned masters Croc and Ox.

Van Damme, playing Croc, has one scene with Peacock when he was captured and threatened with the destruction of the city if he tried to fight back, one more scene with Po and the Furious Five where he and Ox refused to be broken out of prison, and then they were in the final battle where they both decided to fight back and helped Po to beat Peacock and save China.

Overall, his role was small, less than 10 minutes of screen time, some of that just with him being there, and since it's an animated role, he had nothing to do with the character when it wasn't speaking. It was only Van Damme's second voice acting role, the first being in a single episode of *Robot Chicken* two years prior. Other than an even smaller role in *Kung Fu Panda 3*, he's only done one other voice role, in *Minions: The Rise of Gru*, since. Clearly his voice acting career never took off, possibly because he struggles to enunciate at times. Unless the character calls for that distinct broken English, he's likely passed over for more polished voice actors.

- Dave Herndon

Assassination Games (2011)

If there was truth in advertising, *Assassination Games* wouldn't be called an "action" film. It would be called a "boredom" film. I realize that line isn't particularly clever, but it's as qualitative as anything in this film. But I have to hand it to the filmmakers—the film's boredom is an effective moneymaker. What, you ask? How can boredom make money? Well, allow me to explain. Upon taking this assignment, I went to Amazon Prime, located *Assassination Games*, and downloaded it for the too-steep cost of $3.99. I then watched fifteen minutes of it and got bored, shutting it off. "I'll come back to this later," I said. Well, two days passed before I could get back to it, and by that time my rental had expired. This meant I had to spend an additional $3.99, which, as I said, was too much to begin with. This is why I say *Assassination Games'* boringness may be its money-making brilliance. By being so boring, the filmmakers milked the cost of an additional rental out of me.

The big selling point of this movie is that it pits two action stars, Jean-Claude Van Damme and Scott Adkins, against each other in a match-up literally no one was clamoring for (aside from maybe them). How can that go wrong? And yet it does. The two don't even meet until about forty minutes into the movie and then, just as quickly as they became adversaries, they become friends and team up. And neither of their mothers is even named Martha! (If you don't get this lame joke, Google it)

And let's be honest, is Scott Adkins really an action star on the level of JCVD? Not a knock against Adkins, but at one time Van Damme was a real movie star. One who made movies that actually played in theaters. Whereas Adkins is best known for straight-to-DVD sequels to action movies that had actual stars in them. But, by this point in Van Damme's career, everything he was making was going to straight-to-Redbox, too, so

I suppose it's a close-to-equal pairing. And for the record, the two would team up again the following year in a straight-to-DVD sequel, *Universal Soldier: Day of Reckoning*. And Sylvester Stallone, one of the "real" action stars who make "real" movies would later ask each of them to appear in his *Expendables* movies. Again, Van Damme makes sense, and it was really good to see him pop up there. But I think we can credit Adkins' appearance as being part of Stallone's searching high and low for more action "stars" to pack in there. I mean, Christ, there are only so many of them to pick from. After that you've gotta go to a nearby QuikTrip and just start recruiting customers. Like Scott Adkins.

Neither actor is particularly good or bad here, just blandly good enough. But then, when you're in a movie that's so bland that no one will remember watching it by the time the last of the credits have rolled, that's probably the fitting type of performance. In fact, the director may have actually instructed them to be bland. "Hey, listen, Jean, you're kind of standing out a little there. It was good, but I'm afraid someone might watch that and actually remember your performance, and by default the movie, ten minutes after it's over. So, we're gonna shoot that scene again, and I'm gonna need you to dial it back a bit to, say, room temperature. Or better yet, how about this? When you're doing the scene, just think about what elevator music sounds like and then try to be that. Become the elevator music. Can you do that?"

As for the director, I kid. Look, the director, Ernie Barbarash, isn't bad. He's actually a decent filmmaker. His style is slightly pedestrian and he's one of those journeyman directors who direct a lot of sequels and then end up making Christmas movies. And that's fine. Do you know how many wannabe directors there are out there who would literally kill to direct one movie, let alone the number Barbarash has? And you know what? He was a co-producer on two really great films, *American Psycho* and *The Cat's Meow*. But this one isn't so great.

If we want to blame someone, let's blame the screenwriter, Aaron Rahsaan Thomas, who wrote this thing like an episode of a bland procedural cop show with nothing but letters in its title. Hmm. Let's look up his credits and see what else he's written... Oh, lots of episodes of *S.W.A.T.* and *CSI: NY*. Okay, that makes sense.

The movie looks okay, though. It doesn't look bright and flashy like a Jerry Bruckheimer movie, but it also doesn't look terrific like Vilmos Zsigmond or Roger Deakins shot it. It looks clear and the filmmakers used that filter all the cheap action movies were using around that time that makes it look kind of orangey and washed out. Kind of cool in a no-budget sort of way, so the movie at least has that going for it.

The truth of the matter is this movie isn't even bad. It's nothing. It's as bland as a mayonnaise sandwich on generic white bread. It's the kind of movie you actually wish was bad just so you could feel something. Literally anything besides boredom. Who are these characters and what are their names? You've been watching it for over an hour, and you have no idea what their names are, and you don't give a damn. By this point you just want it to be over.

The only takeaway from Assassination Games was that this was the first time I ever noticed that JCVD had a giant bulge on his forehead. What the hell is that? A tumor? In my head I hear Schwarzenegger saying, *"It's a tooooomah!"* And then, suddenly, I'm slightly concerned about his health, which becomes the first and only thing about this movie I've given the slightest fuck about.

- Andrew J. Rausch

Beur sur la ville (2011)

JCVD likes his cameo appearances but only this one, to the best of my knowledge, features him delivering his patented high kicks while wearing a burqa. You know that big black garment that covers the entire bodies of women in certain Islamic traditions. Let that sink in and I'll continue.

Or maybe not. Do I really need to say anything more? Is that a thousand words, David? Not quite? OK...

Just in case that wild visual doesn't make it particularly clear, *Beur sur la ville*, or *Arab on the City*, is a French police comedy and it's worth pointing out that French police comedies are not like any other nation's police comedies. For instance, I could compare this to the *Police Academy* series, if I was feeling vicious, because it's about inept cops bumbling their way towards the solution of a high-profile crime. However, I'd need to apologise to writer/director Djamel Bensalah, because, for all the flaws that his movie has, it's a heck of a lot better than them. French police comedies may contain copious amounts of French, police and comedy, but they also tend to use their platforms to tell actual stories that have actual value and actual social commentary, and this one is no exception.

Someone is murdering young women in the Villeneuve district of Paris and they're extra brutal about it. There's decapitation with a sword or scimitar. There's frenzied mutilation of the corpses. And there's postmortem rape. They're also doing it in the Muslim district, which makes it fair for journalists to hassle Governor Flaubert at his press conference to present the new batch of all white graduates from the academy and ask if there's someone who might be better equipped to handle murders near mosques. Governor Flaubert promptly tells the State Commissioner that he wants "some colour out there" to head up the Friday Killer case.

The catch is that the people tasked with locating that colour have every intention of sabotaging the Governor's re-election, so they locate the worst candidates imaginable. Enter Henry Tong and Mamadou Koulibali, new Police Officers, and Khalid Belkacem, new Lieutenant. Belkacem is our lead, and he just failed the officer exam with panache. He thought xenophobia was the fear of insects. He's allergic to everything. He's also a foot shorter than Diane Dardenne, the Crime Squad captain he'll work alongside.

This trio's experience with policework has been restricted to pulling over cars to settle bets as to whether they're a Mercedes 300 or a 600SL, so you can imagine how well this doesn't go. Khalid can't drive so recruits his granddad to transport him to the next crime scene. Mamadou faints when he sees the corpse.

But, as I'm sure you guessed already, Khalid also manages to provide some honest-to-goodness help, much to the surprise of Crime Squad. Sure, to play into the colourful metaphors this movie uses to highlight stereotypes, he's as useless as a pork sandwich at a mosque fundraiser, but he knows the area and its people and how everything functions. So he sees things that don't add up and a colourful set of supporting characters, who will only talk to locals, shed light on these things and suddenly there's progress.

And that brings us to JCVD, because that's who you really care about, not the lead clowns, however funny they sometimes are. And JCVD is extra-funny because he's Le Colonel. The clues point to an army captain, Christophe Roi, so they ask an army buddy about him and that's Le Colonel, an ultra-tough military instructor who alternates his time between throwing unwilling soldiers out of a tower as some sort of parachute training and complaining about how "This army has no more soldiers. Only faggots." He dismisses the idea that Capt. Roi had murdered three women in Afghanistan by pointing out that, I kid you not, "The three dead women had ambushed our men."

This isn't the first time we see JCVD but it's the first time we *see* him, if that makes sense. His earlier action scenes have him utterly hidden within that burqa, which must be pretty restrictive clothing when it comes to using martial arts against cops on the roof of a mosque or, indeed, jumping off that roof to escape when the guns come out to play. I'd love to know if these scenes were actually van Damme or just a random stuntman. After all, in that costume, it could have been me, right? Maybe it was.

Given that this film is only streaming on a website in French and the only English subtitles I could find don't quite match the edit and unfold at a slightly different speed, I'm going to assume that you're never going to see it and so I can spoil away. JCVD is not, I repeat not, the Friday Killer. He's just the local drug lord whose dealers are the young ladies being killed. We learn this right after he leaves a women's football game, still clad from head to toe in his burqa, on a motorcycle and drives it right into a police car. He spends the next scene heavily bandaged and heavily cooperative. Capt. Roi must be the killer, he thinks. He converted to Islam in prison, becoming Ben Ali. "Since he got his dick trimmed," he suggests, "he's a changed man."

I liked this movie and not just because Jean-Claude van Damme has a bundle of fun being wildly inappropriate. The whole movie is wildly inappropriate, but with a heart. There's depth here if you pay attention to what's really going on, why the stereotypes and the clichés. And hey, being French, it goes where police comedies don't go anywhere else. It doesn't hold back from racial slurs—a pivotal character keeps calling Arabs "sand niggers"—and, while it's hardly *Seven*, it's happy to get brutal. You don't see anyone killed with a nail gun in *Police Academy*. And you don't see JCVD kicking ass as a ninja in a burqa.

- Hal CF Astell

6 Bullets (2012)

I liked this latter-day Jean-Claude van Damme movie until, well, I didn't.

Initially, it's a lot deeper than the typical action flick, as the title, referencing a quote, suggests: "Modern day slavery is big business. I once saw a child sold for six bullets and I did nothing." That angle is a brutal one to explore on film, but there's a more brutal one about to unfold, one that flavours the first half of the movie.

We open in a brothel full of beautiful but bored women. Clearly, we're in eastern Europe and the cast list suggests Romania. JCVD is there, wearing a goatee and glasses, like he's the sort of mildly intellectual Lenin clone you might order on Wish. Everyone's taller than he is. Security is everywhere. We realise that we're in a specialist area of the brothel when the women become girls, very young girls. JCVD is Young@Heart_69 and he's paying handsomely for an hour with a little boy.

Before that happens, the boss gets a call. The boy has a rich cousin in America who paid someone very special a lot of money to bring him home. I wonder who that might be! And JCVD is not messing around here! He kills everyone: one with acid, a bunch with knives. He locates little Victor, removes his fake facial hair and they escape by motorbike. Cue lots of explosions.

And, as we're cheering him on, the mood shifts. His source of information is seriously pissed. Sure, Victor's safe but what about the others? Apparently, the bad guys have a habit of hiding child prostitutes in the walls when they realise a raid is happening. Those explosions JCVD set outside spread and took down the building. They're all dead. We see a couple of them: girls, maybe nine or ten years old. The cop tells him to go home and leave policework to the police. He kind of has a point.

Now that this movie has skewered the unfettered vigilantism that fuels so many other action movies, we shift focus. An American family arrive at the airport in Chisinau, Moldova. They're the Faydens: Andrew and Monica and their cute daughter, Becky, who's fourteen with blue eyes and blonde hair. She's so cute she even poses for photos in the street. And she's so green that she's taken from their hotel by the nice lady stranger whom she didn't realise was also snapping pics.

And that prompts quite the manhunt, because Andrew Fayden is an MMA champion. He has the neck tattoos and everything. His promoter flaunts a $10k reward. The family doubles it. And JCVD is watching. The Faydens come to see him, at the butcher's shop he runs now that he's retired from accidentally blowing up kids. They want Samson Gaul, who was recommended to them by the man from the embassy. "He's dead," says JCVD. "The man you're looking for is no longer here." He's Samson Gaul, naturally, and he's busy drinking vodka, wallowing in self-pity and seeing visions of the girls he burned in the brothel.

The nice lady who steals away young girls is Bianca van Varenberg. The man from the embassy is Kristopher van Varenberg. JCVD, of course, is Jean-Claude van Varenberg. This is a family affair, his kids on both sides of what is clearly big business in Moldova. Everyone else is used to travelling light years further than eastern Europe. Well, the Faydens, at least. Andrew is Joe Flanigan, who was Lt. Col. John Sheppard in *Stargate: Atlantis*. Monica is Anna-Louise Plowman, who was Osiris on *Stargate: SG-1*. Whether that's a coincidence, I have no idea, but they're both welcome, at least until the movie changes.

It won't surprise that the Faydens want their kid back and they're going to go to serious lengths to make that happen. It shouldn't surprise that Samson Gaul joins them on this quest, because maybe doing it right for once might make the visions go away. And it can't be much of a surprise to find that this story, so good at highlighting a downside to vigilantism, suddenly becomes a vigilante action movie. One minute, Samson Gaul is tortured by his failures as a vigilante. The next, he has a large arsenal.

Is that a rocket launcher? Cool! Yeah, to suggest this is a schizophrenic movie is an understatement.

The good news is that there are surprises. I particularly liked that, as much as Becky's dad is an MMA champion expected to kick ass and take names, he's not emasculated by the fact that it's mum who has the cojones in the family. It's Monica who's willing to rip off a doctor's balls to get him to talk. It's Monica who's willing to kill to save her daughter.

Unfortunately, there are also plot consistency issues, need for suspension of disbelief and a location problem. The big city is cool and corrupt and claustrophobic, but we end up in the middle of nowhere for a clear battle between good guys and bad guys, which is disappointing. This is far from JCVD's worst, but it's also not close to his best, even if Samson Gaul's return to action is acutely memorable.

Andrew searches for his daughter in the red-light district and is pointed to the Golden Girls Club. He starts a fight and, after finally getting knocked down, out go the lights and in comes someone in a mask with infrared goggles. This may be a way to justify using a stunt double for JCVD, now that he's fifty-two, but it works well. Oh, and why JCVD and not the MMA champion? Because nobody ever sees him coming. He has cool gadgets, like a pen containing a hypodermic needle that he can use to get into places. He can rig elaborate traps for people in their own homes in a blink of an eye, like MacGyver on speed.

And that may be the best way to remember this movie. Even if it's completely wrong.

- Hal CF Astell

Rzhevskiy protiv Napoleona (2012)

Let me preface this by saying I watched it with its original Russian language and no subtitles, so the majority of this is using visual cues. This movie is a comedy, and it is a raunchy film. Before we hit the five-minute mark, we see Napoleon take a woman into a tower and it is implied that sex with him is so active, it's why the tower of Pisa leans. It's a dumb joke and I am surprised JCVD would do such a movie, but I digress. I am a huge fan of slapstick and raunchy humor, so I had a blast. If I did acid, this would be a perfect movie to trip to. There are visual jokes aplenty, and I know I lost a lot of the verbal humor in the movie, but I couldn't take my eyes of the visual insanity I was subjecting myself to. This movie was a rapid-fire attack on the eyes.

This is one of those films you watch with the sound off and admire things on a technical scale, for the most part. There is a small magic carpet ride throughout a building where things get knocked down, it was a decent effect for the small budget they had. There was also some terrible green screen stuff that happens, but I think the entire effects budget went to the magic carpet and rocking the Tower of Pisa. This movie is the Russian version of leave your brain at the door. I left my brain at the door, and it took some guessing to figure out a plot of trying to seduce Napoleon. I could tell that the man hired to seduce Napoleon falls for a woman. I also want to know why the song "Like a Virgin" is used. It's used in the English version but instead of a rock song, its sung softer, almost like a 50's crooner. It's an interesting take on the song, but not sure what purpose it serves.

The direction is great, there is a lot of choreography that needs to happen, and it's executed well. The camera movements are fluid, and it looks like it had a decent production value. The film has an "anything goes" style to its filmmaking, and sometimes that's great, other times it's difficult to watch. One scene that is worth the rental, or at least the time to watch it, is the way they take what is supposed to be a formal dance and turn it on its head using provocative dancing with sexual moves. It also goes outside the period piece story using dance moves that I would not associate with that time period. A unique interpretation. That said, the period costumes were amazing. They looked authentic and I can tell they put some time into them. I wish I had more to say about it, but it is a period piece, so you know they are going to put the effort in and making the actors look good. There is a scene where they have some sort of fashion show and you see an homage to *The Fifth Element*, I chuckled at that one and it made me want to see what I can do about finding the dubbed version.

The only truly horrid aspect of the movie is the editing. Sometimes scenes are so quick and there are a couple of inserts that only last 1-2 seconds, so it doesn't make a difference in terms of the story, but in the pacing, it throws it right off. There are scenes that are sped up for comedic relief, but the rest seems sloppy and bit too quick.

Regarding Jean-Claude Van Damme, his scene comes when the man hired to dress as a woman to seduce Napoleon goes into JCVD's room, and they talk about him stealing Jean-Claude's pants. I do want to say that Jean-Claude looks his most ridiculous in this movie. He doesn't have the body for period pieces and his hair just looks weird. His character's name is also Jean-Claude Van Damme as part of a joke, so the absurdity is there. I am suggesting this because he says that name in the dialogue. There is also a brief moment where they speak English and the character wants Van Damme's clothes to impress a woman, they have a fight, and the guy who is not Van Damme wins (which shows that this is a comedy).

It's nice to see Jean-Claude in a 100% comedy. He does the action movies with comedic lines, but this one is just farce and it's weird, wacky, confusing, but visually interesting. I appreciate that JCVD seems to be in on the jokes about his fighting and his masculinity, all of which are appreciated. His role is a cameo, but he makes the most of it and it is a highlight.

I can't tell if I liked this movie a lot, but I will be talking about it to my circle of friends. I would love to see this movie get an American remake and have Jean-Claude reprise his role as the same character. It's nice to see how sex comedies are done in other countries. I thought that America was raunchy, however Russia comes close. The runtime doesn't even cross 80 minutes before credits, which is either great or a disappointment, depending on your enjoyment level. If you are interested in seeing Jean Claude in a comedic movie, you should look elsewhere as he's not in this one much. If you want to see a weird ass movie with *Airplane!*-like jokes and visual storytelling and from another country, this is it.

- Stephen Kessen

Dragon Eyes (2012)

Jean-Claude Van Damme is back in prison again and this time he never leaves. No, that's not a spoiler. It really doesn't matter that much because he's hardly in the movie. He's Tiano and he's only here to be the mentor and trainer of the main character in a set of flashback scenes. He looks able, his balance effortless and his kicks powerful, but the brushed steel color palette makes him look a lot older than he was. I've seen more recent films in which he looked younger than this.

At least what little time he gets is action-packed. It wouldn't surprise me to discover that he was only on set for one day as a favor to director John Hyams's dad, Peter, who had previously directed him in *Timecop* and the excellent *Sudden Death*. Certainly, JCVD only interacts with a single primary cast member and all, but his first scene unfolds in a single prison cell.

That first scene involves him stepping in to end a fight with a serious kick. A massive fellow inmate is picking on a young Chinese prisoner, who's ballsy enough to respond physically when it's clear a fight will happen. He isn't remotely able, and he gets his ass kicked, but he apparently did enough to show Tiano that he has the dragon eyes of the title, which translates from the spiritually obscure to something like "containing enough goddamn stubbornness to be worthy of being trained by JCVD".

That cast member is Cung Le, a Vietnamese wrestler and martial artist who has held world titles in kickboxing, tae kwon do, and MMA. Le punches and kicks very hard and I'd love to see him fight similar hard hitters like Tony Jaa and Iko Uwais. He also has a presence to him, which ought to serve him well in the movies, if perhaps more often as a villain than the antihero he plays here.

The worst aspect to Cung Le is that he displays very little emotion, which limits his abilities as an actor but actually plays into his role here. We eventually learn that his name is Hong, but he's really the archetypal Man with No Name character. Maybe half this movie unfolds like Yojimbo (or its spaghetti western remake, *A Fistful of Dollars*) translated to American gangland, meaning that he's the new guy in St. Jude, wherever the heck St. Jude is, and he stirs things up between two rival gangs so that they'll wipe each other out in a turf war and thus restore peace and civility to everyone else. Why he does this isn't clear but it's some sort of redemption.

What changes from that classic template is that it becomes clear that it just isn't going to fly. Sure, Hong can set the irascible cholos of the 6th St. Kings and the more thoughtful yardies, the Eastsiders, at each other's throats, because they're so easily manipulated that my grandkids could probably do it and I don't just mean the ones old enough to attend school. However, St. Jude isn't remotely as isolated as the villages in those aforementioned movies, so that the Lord Devil Dogs, who look British but might be Russian, are always ready to step in. They run the territory next door and are open to expansion. They serve as able wildcards.

The biggest reason, though, is that there's one man above both gangs, who's in charge of everything that happens in St. Jude, to the degree that he alone can hold the Lord Devil Dogs at bay. He's Victor Swan, known to all and sundry as Mister V, and there are two reasons why he's firmly at the top of the food chain. One is that he's a cop, so he has forces to bring to bear that the gangsters don't. The other is that he's played by Peter Weller with serious relish. Mister V can walk unarmed into a heated argument between the leaders of "the spics and the schwarzes", abuse them both and not one of us in the cheap seats is going to fail to believe it.

Quite frankly, Weller is the primary reason anyone ought to watch this movie. It isn't the patient artiness of the cinematography. It isn't the Guy Ritchie-esque introductions to characters. It certainly isn't the back story because I'm not sure even writer Tim Tori had that straight in his head. The reasons to watch are Peter Weller first, second and third with Cung Le and his fight scenes fourth. JCVD is probably fifth and he's hardly in the damn film. Sixth has to be Sari Cummings as Honey Darling, a hooker with seriously dangerous nipples whose domination of Sgt. Howe is interrupted by Mister V trying to figure out who stole his money; he teaches her how to punch his henchman properly and she enjoys the lesson. Seventh is brutality, because none of the punches in this film seem pulled, whether they're thrown by or at Cung Le. Eighth is a drinking game: take a shot whenever an actor on screen has a cauliflower ear. Prediction: you'll die.

Anyway, with Mister V in charge, Hong isn't going to win using the Yojimbo method, so the film changes into something else and I wish I had a clue what Tori had in mind for the second half. I was OK with it until a wildly disappointing finalé, which attempts to wrap up every loose end in one brief scene with a very abrupt ending, as if the production had just run out of time and so ripped the entire third act out of the script. I can hear the director shouting at the writer, "Screw it! We have enough budget left to light one scene, so let's just have everyone still alive who has any meaning in this story show up in the same place at the same time so they can mostly shoot each other dead in the world's largest Mexican standoff! That's a wrap! Fade to credits."

- Hal CF Astell

The Expendables 2 (2012)

In Memory of Jean Vilain

Jean Vilain, né Sébastien Michels, 52, died August 12, 2012 from injuries sustained from an altercation over found property in Albania. Jean Vilain was but one man who saw great things arising from conflict, and believe the strongest of mind, body, and heart could overcome any obstacle.

Born Sébastien Michels October 12, 1960 to wealthy Belgian missionaries in the Belgian Congo, he began life following in the solid Christian fellowship of his parents, Gilbert and Sophie, as they spread the good word and specialized prosperity gospel to the simple villagers of their local colony. They both tragically lost their lives in a village uprising when he was 4. Sébastien, and his older brother, Seef, were sent to a boarding school in Switzerland, earning average grades and mostly keeping to themselves. Being the older, Seef stood up for his smaller, weaker brother, fighting most playground battles, until one schoolyard scrum proved fatal for a fellow classmate. Not wanting to see his brother expelled for previous violations, Sébastien selfishly took credit for the death. The family encouraged with assistance from the Michels family fortune to grieve quietly and in another country, and Sébastien and Gilbert experienced the heady rush that came from fostering enthusiastic self-preservation in others. Sébastien graduated with high honors and his transcripts tout his fondness of ballet and economics, earning him the nickname, *En Avant Arbitrage*. It is believed he gave that nickname to himself as it made little sense to anyone else.

Sébastien traveled the world in search of a purpose, surviving on his charm and his vast inheritance. He joined the Belgian military rising to a mid-grade supply clerk, mostly overseeing the supply train and managing the logistics and movement of large groups of personnel and units from one base to another. Through what was determined to be a clerical error and no fault of his own, munitions mysteriously disappeared on route to be decommissioned. It is believed Sébastien mistakenly thought he would take the blame and went AWOL, never to be seen or known as Sébastien Michels again. The tanks were later found abandoned and striped in a Belgian ghetto, likely misrouted. Enlisted men were also found inside a local bar sleeping off a week-long party paid for by the sale of parts from the tanks. Records show the Belgian Army never made an effort to track Sébastien Michels down or return him to duty.

Sébastien took odd jobs to keep stave off boredom as an office job or military career never seemed like a food fit. He spent 5 years in a traveling ballet troupe touring the former Soviet Union, and his portrayal of the Wolf in Prokofiev's Peter and the Wolf is today still unmatched in its realism and brutality.

There was a joyous reunion as he again teamed up with his older brother, Seef, who had changed his name to Claude Vilain. Sébastien then changed his name to "Jean" and took his brothers new surname, as he believed "Naughty John" suited him quite well and together they joined the French Foreign Legion, fighting in the Chadian-Libyan conflict during the late 1980s. Together they became a team of Robin Hood-style vigilante spreading their goodwill and employment opportunities throughout Eastern Europe. They were once again separated and Jean struck out on his own. His rise through the ranks of Belgium's legitimate businessmen come mostly after a series of accidents and unfortunately gang wars between his employers and rival enterprises. Sébastien often found himself the last man standing and pooled his resources.

Surfacing in Albania in 2012, Jean he was the head and main financier of unpolished tradesmen skilled in firearms and subterfuge, known as The Sangs, or "The Bloods", an homage to the US-based street gang, known for its unfortunate, but violently provoked confrontations. Drawing on his wealth and knowledge of the international banking system, he personally trained Sangs and provided every member with only the best military-grade weaponry and body armor. He brilliantly consolidated the smaller organizations he'd acquired through attrition and expanded his enterprises into pharmacology, hospitality and security, companionship services for a lonely clientele, and professional retrieval and disposal services

Jean Vilain believed himself to be the best as broker for the job when he discovered an abandoned cache of Cold War-Era weapons-grade plutonium. Fearing for the safety of mankind should the dangerous materials fall into the wrong hands, he set up an elaborate bidding system to ensure only the richest of society would handle it with the best of care. Sadly while en route, Jean crossed paths with a mercenary black ops ghost team going only by their code name *The Expendables*. In an altercation led by Barney Ross, Jean was goaded into killing a member of The Expendables, a young man by the name of Billy the Kid who was only his final mission before heading home to be with his fiancée. That unprovoked death would prove to be linchpin in Jean's unfortunate death, and the Expendables invoked a death curse, and chased him and his business associates all over Albania. While defending himself in an airport, he suffered multiple and fatal contusions and fractures and the hands of Barney Ross. Tragically, his head has never been found.

The remains of Jean Vilain will be interred in the Michels Family crypt in beneath *Begraafplaats van Laken* (Laeken Cemetery) in Brussels, Belgium. He will lie beside the remains of his parents. There will be a private memorial service held for surviving family with a light repast to follow. In lieu of flowers, Claude Vilain would like donations made to the Save the World Charity, which when is funded to the total of $2B (USD), the world will be saved from nuclear annihilation. His Belgian Bank account is BE25621260437503. You have 48 Hours from the publication of this obituary.

If anyone can produce the head of Jean Vilain, that individual plus up to 5 family members or close associates, will be granted safe passage to the villa of their choice upon validation prior to the 48-hour deadline.

May the odds be ever in your favor.

- Montilee Stormer

UFO: Alien Uprising (2012)

The first question you're going to ask yourselves while watching the opening scenes of *UFO*, or *Alien Uprising*, to use its more active retitle, is "What the heck is this?"

Is it an edgy handheld military action movie? Is it a cheesy alien abduction flick? Is it a teenybopper Coachella romance? It appears to be all those things and ironically isn't any of them.

What it certainly isn't is a Jean-Claude van Damme movie. He's in it, or you wouldn't be reading this, and his is the first face we see, but he's only there during unexplained flashbacks that are shot in a different grain until late in the movie, when it seems like he's about to join the fray and then doesn't. Sorry.

Whose film is it? Well, the names we recognise all show up at the end of the opening credits: "with Sean Pertwee", "with Julian Glover", "and Jean-Claude van Damme". The star is nominally Bianca Bree, as Carrie, and the most prominent role is given to Sean Brosnan as Michael.

And that really boils down to it being a movie full of kids, not through age but through relationships. Bianca Bree is Jean-Claude van Damme's daughter. Sean Brosnan is Pierce Brosnan's son. Sean Pertwee is Jon Pertwee's son. So, this film could have starred JCVD, James Bond and the Third Doctor, but it really stars their offspring. Sorry.

This is an indie drama, the sort you might see at a film festival light enough on strong submissions to accept something for the draw of name recognition. It clearly didn't have a large budget, hence the focus away from an alien invasion towards a bunch of everyday people who happen to notice it. The tagline may read "The real 'battle' is the insurgence within mankind itself" because writer/director Dominic Burns felt a burning need to hurl incisive social commentary against the backdrop of a world-changing event, but it's more likely to be a translation of "we don't have a special effects budget".

It's mostly conversational, with all the key characters staying at Robin's house in a small town north of London. Wikipedia tells me it's Derby but, unless I blinked at the wrong moment, the script didn't. Robin's a former soldier who proposes to his girlfriend, Dana, outside a club. His friends, Michael and Vincent, are inside, trying to pull birds. Michael, maybe boosted by the confidence that comes with being an officer in the S.A.S., pulls Carrie, who's American. Vincent just pukes over his target and gets thrown out.

It tries to be edgy, not just through the ensuing fight with the club's bouncers but through the bizarre alternation between a couple of sex scenes and Vincent throwing up in the toilet. Now, they're not the greatest sex scenes in history, but that's a surefire way to defuse our reaction to them. I'm sure the point is to just ground us in the everyday lives of these characters, ahead of them walking outside in the morning to find that the world has changed.

How? Well, there's no electricity, no radio and no reception on their phones. The awful newsreader the night before said that there was nothing to worry about, but the neighbour's wife has been called to an emergency meeting in London. She's part of the British government's Domestic Crisis Response unit. And then they bump into what seems to be an apocalyptic vagrant, played with relish by Sean Pertwee with a cross between his eyes. It's the end of times, he says, apparently citing Biblical references.

And, after a couple more conversational scenes, there's a spaceship hanging in the air outside. It continues to hang there, and we do wonder how long it's going to hang there while this movie happens around it.

I could be generous and say that a bunch of stuff happens, but it really doesn't. There are some fights around supermarkets as a panicked populace attempts to prep. Julian Glover has a strong but pessimistic scene as a garage owner. There is one excellent action scene, between Michael and a cop who is presumably not really a cop. It's shot in jagged fashion, but the cop has fantastic moves. The actor is Joey Ansah, who had made his name as an assassin fighting Matt Damon in *The Bourne Ultimatum*. He's a student of taekwondo, ninpo taijutsu, capoeira and hip-hop dance. I wish he'd have got a fight here with JCVD but it doesn't happen. Sorry.

And, talking of JCVD, he's George and he knows things: "military, black ops, you name it". Whoever's left alive at this point goes to visit him to see what he can tell them about whatever's going on and he can tell them plenty. His sudden actual presence in the film, as against a succession of teasing flashbacks, coincides with a change in what it wants to be. Suddenly it's an action movie and the aliens show up and there's a space battle in the sky and... while I realise that movies don't tend to be shot in order, it feels acutely like they shot 90% of this one then discovered that they had a budget after all.

There's more testosterone than action because there are a lot more testosterone scenes than action scenes. Some of them make sense. Some are a real stretch. There's the most ridiculous attempted rape scene that I've ever watched, surely there to highlight how our true selves will emerge in a crisis, this being as extreme a crisis as it gets, even if most of it is offscreen.

I'd say that there's a good movie in here struggling to get out, but it doesn't struggle particularly hard. A budget would certainly have helped, but it needed a lot of changes to become what it could have been. But hey, JCVD gets vaporized by aliens! How often does that happen? Oh, and that's no spoiler. However, the best thing about the movie is, so I can't tell you about it. Sorry.

- Hal CF Astell

Universal Soldier: Day of Reckoning (2012)

Imagine taking your favorite Ben & Jerry's and Haagen Dazs flavors, maybe a dozen in total, and putting all of them into a blender. When it's all done, you pour it out in all of its multi-colored kaleidoscope of lumpy textures and what you get is pretty fantastic. You can taste the *Cherry Garcia*, then the *Deep Chocolate Peanut Butter*...a piece of cone from *Cameral Cone*! Then, yum, there's a hint of *Strawberry Cheesecake* and then, wow! There's the *Phish Food*!

You're well aware that the whole ridiculous ice cream experiment doesn't really work, but who cares...it's an indulgent escapade of utter gluttony. You keep taking long sips of it, relishing in how over-the-top it is. Though the whole time you're wondering if you should just throw the whole concoction down the sink, as it's just too grossly ridiculous and disgustingly complex. But you just keep gulping it down because it's just too much fun.

This is kind of what it was like watching *Universal Solder: Day of Reckoning*. Lots of crazy violence and all sorts of plot twists lumped in with so many of my all-time favorite paranoidal thrillers all in one big movie blender.

I'll go through a few of them in chunks (*Chunky Monkey*-style).

Let's start with the *Manchurian Candidate*, the Denzel version. The distressed veteran soldiers who were victims of brainwashing ate instant noodles. In *Day of Reckoning*, similarly brainwashed soldiers instead swigged bottles of bourbon. Both groups of traumatized veterans in each movie had implants they extracted from their bodies.

Day of Reckoning seemed to employ the same psycho artist that created those haunting images in 2004's *Manchurian Candidate* remake. And it had an eerily similar creepy mad scientist doctor who coincidentally led an even more eerily similar secret mind control program. I bet the filmmakers of *Manchurian Candidate* probably felt the same way Jimmy Page did when he saw the Whitesnake guitarist pull out a violin bow to play a guitar solo.

Throw in a bunch of false memories and aforementioned implants to extract, and there's yet another great sci fi movie that comes to mind: Paul Verhoeven's paranoidal classic *Total Recal*

And if you wanted to see a knock-off of the replicants from *Blade Runner*, the UniSol humanoid/clone/assassins in *Day of Reckoning* were serviceable stand-ins, just not as personable. Or pretty. Remember Daryl Hannah?

As the whiskey-boozing haunted and shattered soldiers continue to deteriorate from a rogue government program gone bad, I couldn't help but think of one of my other all-time favorite paranoidal thrillers, *Jacob's Ladder.* Well, just minus all the demonology.

Other film writers have mentioned *Angel Heart, Chinatown, Mulholland Drive, The Big Sleep, Into the Void, All the President's Men* and many others as major influences on *Day of Reckoning*. According to interviews, Hyams has cited a few of these films plus *Invasion of the Body Snatchers* as inspirations for the film. Some he borrowed from so brazenly with his own little twist, like those hilarious whiskey bottles, that you can only just laugh at it all with an approving nod.

Everything the filmmakers of *Day of Reckoning* took, stole, sampled, co-opted, were inspired by XXX (whatever label you want to throw on it) based on what type of film snob you are, it's just all good. It ain't a rip-off if it's an inspiration. The movie just winds up being as much fun as indulging in all of your favorite ice creams at once.

And what's wrong with a rip-off anyway? I've certainly been in a few as an actor. I was in perhaps one of the most infamous knock-off movies ever made, *The Amazing Bulk*. And I was in a *Saw* rip-off, too. And a *Black*

Dahlia one. And an *Iron Man* one. (Damn how many of these have I really been in? Maybe I should get back to the subject at hand).

Sometimes I think the entire straight-to-DVD market wouldn't even exist if it wasn't for these kinds of knock-off movies propping it all up. It's a marketing and promotional bonanza for smaller production companies to find a gimmicky angle to make a buck. It creates jobs.

I could go on and on with more movies I think Hyams threw into the blender, but I have only been allotted a thousand words in this essay to get my point across. So, I'll just talk about the one movie where the nod to a great movie, well....it gave me a real crick in my neck. And it might've also spoiled the multi-ice cream concoction I was enjoying so much. Well, it almost did.

Jean-Claude Van Damme as Col. Kurtz from *Apocalypse Now.*

Yes, you read right. It was unmistakable. Now, this quirky director of *Day of Reckoning* might deny it, but I have a feeling he'd have a sense of humor about the whole thing. He might even laugh about the fact that he even had soldiers go visit him up the river by boat, just like Martin Sheen and company did in Francis Ford Coppola's masterpiece.

But still.

Joking aside.

Van Damme as Col. Kurtz!? Really!?

It's just a little too hard to swallow. Kinda like Ben & Jerry's *Schweddy Balls*. Never did like that one too much. You had me up until then, John Hyams. I was rooting for you! Defending all of your rip offs. I mean 'inspirations'.

Oh well. I still adore the movie. No one thought a straight-to-DVD sixth entry in a *Universal Soldier* series infamous for its camp would be this good. The action, the plot twists, the sheer ambition of the movie was the real 'inspiration' here. John Hyman threw in so many of my favorite movies into one deliciously blended concoction of a sequel that the movie has gained a cult following of sorts over the years.

Marlon Brando is turning in his grave.

- Jed Rowen

Enemies Closer (2013)

For all intents and purposes, *Enemies Closer* is not a great movie. For the most part, it's derivative direct-to-video junk that you'd see permeating one of three places: a.) the $5 DVD bin at Walmart, b.) late night on the SyFy channel or its equivalent (provided that people still watch cable TV), or c.) its predominant home on one of the many free streaming services that are funded by way of ads. To my recollection, the latter is where I've seen *Enemies Closer* pop up most. And by all accounts, it's a film that is fairly deserving of its status as one of the many action titles available on Tubi, Freevee, Pluto, etc. However, there are a few aspects with *Enemies Closer* that are worthy of a second look, especially for Jean-Claude Van Damme completists.

Enemies Closer was the third collaboration between Van Damme and esteemed director, Peter Hyams. As of this writing, it stands as Hyams' most recent directing job, and for the most part, it's a competent film that delivers a number of requisite action sequences, and gets in and out within a brisk 85-minute running time.

From the offset, there's much to appreciate about the film, especially its general conceit.

For one, the idea of Van Damme reteaming with Peter Hyams was indeed exciting, especially for fans of Van Damme. Hyams has a fairly prestigious pedigree of directing credits to his name that have gone down in quite high regards. *Capricorn One*, *Running Scared*, and *Narrow Margin* are just a few. Yet it was the films he did with Van Damme that hold a special regard with so many. Hyams directed *Timecop*, which to this day, stands as one of JCVD's most successful films at the box office. The duo collaborated once again on the *Die Hard*-inspired *Sudden Death*, which had JCVD kickboxing a terrorist in a Penguins mascot costume. Not only were these some of Jean-Claude's most successful films, but they were also a couple of his most mainstream films. These were films that appealed to not just his fans, but to wider audiences as well. In other words, you could have a blast watching *Sudden Death*, and if your mom's in the room, she just also might enjoy it.

Enemies Closer also gives audiences something that's still a bit of a rarity for JCVD completists – Van Damme as the villain. Granted, in 2014, this wasn't entirely a new concept, as 2012's *The Expendables 2* had him playing the primary antagonist (not many fans like to consider his early roles in *No Retreat, No Surrender* and *Black Eagle*, as these films are simply bad). Yet JCVD's villain here, Xander is such an eccentric anomaly that the role stands as not just a right angle in his filmography, but one of his wildest roles to date. Xander is a sadistic leader of a drug cartel who has descended upon a small forest along the US-Canadian border who's looking for lost stash of heroin. Oh yeah, and he's also a vegan. His monologue about his childhood pet goose, Edith, is both hilarious and tragic at the same time. And for the film's ensuing 70 minutes, Xander kickboxes his way through a variety of armed soldiers (dressed as a Canadian mountie no less) and bullies the local forest ranger into helping him find the lost heroin. It's basically a low-budget *Cliffhanger* or even *Surviving the Game*-type concept, where you expect that the hero will be running through the forest, jumping from tree branches, and maybe even jumping off a cliff into the river below.

Unfortunately, the movie never really lives up to its premise. For one, it's filmed digitally (the norm for not just DTV action films, but for most movies today), so its cheapness is pretty apparent. For example, rarely does the action take place during the daytime, but instead at night. You'd think that a lower-budget production would want to make use of natural lighting, but I'm assuming that the mountainous forest locale was not as majestic as the original *First Blood*, so they figured masking the sets in darkness was an easy out. It's disappointing, but thankfully, JCVD is in top form, so it kind of balances out.

What's also frustrating is the supporting cast. Like I said earlier, the main "hero" is Henry – a former Navy Seal turned forest ranger played by Tom

Everett Scott. Scott is a decent actor whose most popular role is arguably Tom Hanks' *That Thing You Do!* But he's not exactly the first person you think of for an action hero. And here he doesn't do much to change that perception. To add some more conflict to the film, Henry is confronted by the brother of a guy who was once under Henry's command played by *Mad TV* alum, Orlando Jones. Jones, who's known as a comedian, goes for a dramatic turn as the disgruntled Clay. Yet once Xander rolls into town, Henry and Clay must put aside their differences to survive Xander's desire for his lost heroin and veganism. I always appreciate actors trying something new and stepping out of their comfort zones when it comes to choosing film roles. But here, the two "good guys" are so clearly out of their league that you have to wonder if Hyams went to various casting agencies and took whatever "names" happened to be available because the shoot was starting in just a week. It's just kind of a shame that when JCVD happens to arrive on set and bring his A-game, he's paired with a few actors who, forgive me for saying this, feel almost beneath a project like this.

And that about sums up the film and remains the main idea I'll keep going back to – Van Damme is easily the best thing about this, and his performance reminds you why he's always been such an enigmatic presence on screen. He's always been a natural star, and while the budgets on his films gradually started shrinking, and he entered the realm of DTV films around the 2000's, his acting managed to actually get *better*. *Enemies Closer* stands as a fine reminder and example of just what he can bring to a film. Sure, there's some odd casting choices, the budgetary limitations are widely apparent, and you're left wanting something a little bit better considering the director who's on board. But it could also be worse.

So, if you're scrolling through Tubi or FreeVee, and you happen to spot *Enemies Closer* alongside some other random Steven Seagal titles, this one has a glimmer of more going for it. Just don't expect to be blown away.

- Sean Malloy

Welcome to the Jungle (2013)

Welcome to the Jungle is not your usual Jean-Claude Van Damme action flick, though his character does rather think that it is. It's a comedy, the precise sort of dumbed down, puerile, cretinous comedy that you might expect Hollywood to release in 2013. It's not particularly funny, even if it did trawl a few grins out of me. However, it turns out to have a surprising value that I emphatically wasn't expecting, and it will undoubtedly stay with me because of that. And because of the tiger. Every movie should have a tiger knocking Jean-Claude Van Damme off a cliff!

We follow the cubicle monkeys at the Crawford Design Group, most of whom hate their jobs even before their boss decrees that they'll be getting on a rickety plane at six o'clock the next morning so a geriatric pilot can fly them to a tropical island. They'll be taking part in Xtreme Storm, a mandatory teamwork wilderness retreat. And now you know where Van Damme comes in, as he's Storm, a certified teamwork instructor who will teach them skills like negotiation, teamwork and leadership. All of which, if his presentation is anything to go by, involve weapons.

Van Damme is an absolute hoot here, because he spends most of his screen time lampooning his stereotypical character. He first appears in fatigues and dark shades, strutting in slo-mo in front of a giant picture reading "Peanut Butter Yummy!" He has no clue about anything but knows exactly how to pose in extra-tough fashion. The Xtreme Storm philosophy appears to be based in large part on that one moment in *Bloodsport* after he beats Bolo Yeung. Action posing. Primal screaming. Owning the moment.

Naturally, he vanishes from the film pretty quickly, because the whole point is that the office workers have to get stranded. The pilot just dies. Van Damme has to be attacked by a tiger. Three times. And yes, the third time is the charm, because its attack takes them both off a cliff into the ocean. Oh, yes indeed! This character could only be killed off in spectacular fashion. Not that he is, because we're only half an hour into the movie at this point and we know that can't be it for a character who's this much fun.

I can't be bothered to introduce most of the other characters, because they're all stereotypes. I'll just mention Chris Meyers and Phil Trager, because they drive the film. Chris is the put upon awkward nice guy. Phil is the arrogant asshole who steals his ideas and takes credit for them. That's about all you need to know. Sure, there's the hottie and the yes man and the crude one and a few others, but they don't really matter, even when Lisa the hottie turns out to be Megan Boone from The Blacklist, actually not being wishy-washy for a change. It's all about Chris and Phil, especially when they lose Storm and have to figure out how to survive on their own, not just themselves but the whole group.

And here's where the unexpected value of this movie comes in.

Chris is a highly experienced Eagle Scout with a portfolio of survival skills. Phil doesn't know anything about anything. When Brenda's bitten by a snake, Chris is able to identify its species from a vague description, thus confirming that it isn't venomous, and he plugs the wound appropriately. Phil wanted to amputate. Chris plans to gather nuts and keep a signal fire manned. Phil wants to eat Javier first, because he's the fattest member of the group. So, which of these two would you elect leader of this temporary tribe?

Yeah, it's a ridiculous question but this stupid 2013 comedy accidentally nails America in 2020. Everything seems to be irrevocably polarized. Either you follow Chris and his attempts to get a radio working so you can call for rescue or you follow Phil and worship him as a god. There's no middle ground whatsoever.

I should emphasize that practically no time unfolds here. It may well be that the entire picture unfolds over the single planned weekend, but Team Phil completely devolves into savagery. They construct a giant statue of

Phil, who's now calling himself Orko the Lawgiver. They wear face paint and have orgies. They wield spears and hurl people into the Pit of Shame. They're even losing the power of speech. Perhaps some of this can be explained by the hallucinogenic that Troy is using to lace the coffee, but surely not much.

How this played in 2013, I have no idea, but it works best as a parody of a national state of affairs that didn't come into effect for another few years. That's certainly how I'll remember it. Phil doesn't say "Make America Great Again" but it's implied.

There aren't any surprises to be found here whatsoever, so it can't be a spoiler to point out that Storm didn't really die in the tiger attack. He's still alive, albeit injured, and he'll return to the story soon enough to continue to be a deliberate dollar store knock-off of the average Jean-Claude Van Damme character. He talks the talk, and he certainly looks the look, but he can't walk the walk and that never ceases to be hilarious. Storm is even scared stiff of needles!

I've long appreciated Van Damme's ability to deconstruct on screen everything he does; this is the comedic opposite of the serious approach he took in *JCVD*. Storm can do every single thing that any Van Damme character can do. Except fight. Storm could play any of his characters, with his muscles, confidence and uncanny ability to pose post-punch while primal screaming into the void. He'd merely need a stunt double for the action scenes. The deliberate genius behind this film is the fact that the production actually cast Jean-Claude Van Damme in this role, and he didn't merely jump onboard but threw himself behind the sheer ridiculousness of it all. Much respect, sir.

- Hal CF Astell

Frenchy (2014)

There are a handful of projects where fans anxiously wait for the finished product to launch only to continue to keep waiting due to delays. The intensity builds up...and fans are hit with something that didn't live up to the hype. A few of these projects spring to mind when they were originally put into development hell – *Chinese Democracy, Duke Nukem Forever*, and *Alien Versus Predator*. But not all delayed projects are a letdown. Here's hoping this JCVD production falls in the latter.

For those that don't know, this is Van Damme's personal pet project. This was written, directed, and funded by him. The weird thing about it? Not too many people know that much about this movie. The IMDb page has been up for some time, claiming the film originates from 2010. The synopsis reads, "A military veteran and former mercenary named Frenchy is haunted by his childhood, as well as his past in the military." As much as Van Damme has put into this film, it honestly doesn't sound that much different than some of his later filmography. What's going on?

First, let's address the title. This film has gone through various titles – including *Full Love, The Eagle Path, Soldiers*, and currently *Frenchy*. Originally, it was claimed that while in production, the title was called Full Love. When screening the film at Cannes in 2010, Van Damme changed the name to The Eagle Path. From reports, the name was changed in hopes to picking up a distributor. Unfortunately, distribution never came.

According to a scene from his reality television series (*Jean-Claude Van Damme: Behind Closed Doors*), Van Damme had mentioned how people liked the film with one exception - no one understood the ending. So, in 2012, he went back to do some re-shoots, changed the ending, and renamed the film to *Soldiers*. But this still wasn't enough to get the product into distribution.

In 2014, the film was shown at the Shanghai International Film Festival, this time as *Full Love*. Once again, there was no news on it being distributed. Four years later, it reappeared at Cannes, but it could still never find the right distributor. Currently, the film has been re-edited (again) and the title changed (again) to *Frenchy*. In a Live Q&A session on one of his social media pages, Van Damme had claimed he was looking for a platform to stream the film. This video came out around the same time as his deal with Netflix was announced. Although one could be led to assume Netflix was picking up the film, there has been no news on it reaching the streaming platform any time soon.

As of 2021, the official website for Rodin Entertainment Limited (the website attached to the project) has a form available for inquiring about distribution of *Frenchy* and other Van Damme projects. It is worth noting that the page hasn't been updated since May 2020 so there is no official way of knowing whether or not the film has been picked up by a distributor or streaming service. Fans will likely find out when JCVD announces it.

The latest news to be found regarding *Frenchy* is from the comment section of a YouTube creator (Viking Samurai) interacting with Josef Cannon, an actor from the film. According to a video uploaded on February 22, 2021 by Viking Samurai, Josef Cannon believes the film was going to see a release in late 2021. However, there has been no updates since the comment was made. Although Van Damme has been very active on social media, he also has been silent when it comes to commenting on a release.

Fans, including myself, have long awaited the film to be released. Although there is not much information online regarding *Frenchy*, there are a few reviews that were originally released in 2010. Unfortunately for Van Damme, the reviews weren't too kind. As for the film itself, the closest anyone can get to seeing it is by watching a handful of trailers on YouTube, which is not enough to give it a fair critique. The trailer matches the synopsis in that it does not seem much different from one of

JCVD's other current films – action, car chases, violence, and martial arts. But from the way some fans are talking about it, it could be something worth waiting for.

Regardless of the situation, we'll continue to wait in anticipation for this film to be released. It is understandable to see how protective he is of this project – it was the first film to involve both of his children and it supposedly contains a message that Van Damme is truly passionate about. However, when all is said and done, I think a majority of fans will end up saying, "Why did it take this long to get released?"

- John Bruske

Swelter (2014)

In *Swelter*, Jean-Claude Van Damme does pretty much the opposite of what he did in *Dragon Eyes* two years earlier. In that film, he was almost a featured extra, appearing only in flashbacks, but he was active for most of his minuscule screen time: punching hard, kicking harder and generally being a bad ass mentor to Cung Le. While there are technically flashbacks in this film too, most of his screen time is in the present and there's plenty of it, but he really doesn't do much with it at all. There's only one scene in which he does any martial arts and then so briefly that you could blink and miss it. Which I did. While there's plenty of opportunity for him to use his skills in other scenes, he simply chooses not to. And, as much as I enjoy JCVD movies, let's face it, he's never going to win an Oscar for his acting.

This time out, he's William Stillman, who starts the film by being released from prison. It was a fair cop this time; he was one of a gang of five armed robbers who took a Las Vegas casino for $10m. Four were caught, even after they ziplined over to the next building to sneak away. Fast forwarding to the present, Stillman and Jackson Boyd are released after serving the majority of their ten-year sentences; Shamus McKane had already escaped; and Henry Jaynes Cole, their leader, is broken out by his compatriots because an additional murder charge landed him life. Now, the gang's back together again and in search of Pike, their fifth who wasn't caught because he was shot in the head during the escape and left for dead.

Why? Well, because he's got the loot!

We've already met Pike, but he's changed, in almost every way except the colour of his skin. It's refreshing to see the lead character in what starts as a crime drama but gradually and effectively becomes a modern day western, be African American, especially as he also represents the side of the law, because he's the current sheriff in the small town of Baker, NV, "the gateway to Death Valley." He's lost his memory, so he has no idea who he is—he's going by Bishop nowadays—let alone where he hid the money, and, when his former compatriots show up in town in search of him, he fails to recognise any of them.

To complicate matters, he has a girlfriend—Carmen—who has a daughter—London, a bored teenager looking for excitement in a town with none to offer, except the Dry Mouth, which appears to be a biker bar and presumably unlicensed brothel. And, while Bishop doesn't recognise Cole and the others, his girlfriend certainly does. Oh hello, subplot! Suddenly, there are perspectives, and we can wonder about the Native American biker gang and the local doctor and ambitious Deputy Ronnie and the wacky Rev. Joshua Stone. Surely some of these have applicable motivations and not just to get Bishop out of office for wanting to shut down Tuesday bingo nights for flouting gambling statutes.

There's a lot of potential here. The plot seems very familiar, especially once the framing of it becomes unmistakably a western. If I haven't actually seen a classic western with this plot, then I've dreamt one instead. Small towns are always good settings for stories like this and it ought to help for this one to be as goddamn hot as you expect right next to Death Valley, hence the film's title. The cast includes some excellent character actors. Heck, there's Tracey Walter in the cast and that always bodes well, but it's Alfred Molina who frankly steals the show as Doc with a well-timed set of down to earth pronouncements.

Sadly, writer/director Keith Parmer doesn't make the best use of all those components, though I have to admit it's fascinating to watch JCVD attempt to be a character actor. His banter with the barmaid at the Dry Mouth is surprisingly fun and he's given the shot at redemption that we think he's been looking for all along. Sweat plays no part in this film and nobody's driven crazy by the heat. Well, crazier, at least! McKane is a whack job to begin with, always getting into trouble, usually while twirling the rattlesnake tail he keeps in his pocket. In the end, it comes down to a showdown, as westerns tend to, stripping another potential opportunity for originality away. If this film is an originality onion, it doesn't have a lot of layers left when it reaches the end credits.

I liked JCVD, though I liked Molina and Arie Verveen more. I liked Lennie James a lot as Pike/Bishop, one man trying to do the right thing against increasingly pessimistic odds, especially as he's not particularly sure why. I like the mild spirituality, mostly explored through an old Indian telling Bishop to take the stone that represents his past bad luck and bury it in the desert. If only he'd done that sooner! The inevitable bar fight is fun, though I'd have preferred it to run longer. I like the bar too, with what looks like a state line running through the stage, which is a couple of old pool tables for dancers to dance on. I loved that they each check in with punched timecards too as they climb onto stage. And I like the final shot of the movie, which reveals to us, but only us, the location of the money that was a MacGuffin to a few early on and eventually a MacGuffin to everyone in town.

It's another experiment, I guess, for Van Damme. I've seen movies where he doesn't do the splits, but I didn't think I'd ever see one where he's a legitimate character actor, who loses the only mano a mano fight he gets into. Respect for trying something new, sir. Shame it didn't work out as well as it might have done.

- Hal CF Astell

Jian Bing Man (2015)

Here's something a little different that I can happily recommend, but with a couple of major caveats.

One is that, while it's possible to enjoy this completely blind, it's such a self-referential nested set of in jokes about the Hong Kong and Chinese film industries that, if you don't know at least something about them, much of this picture is going to fly right over your head. You're going to be like Drax from Guardians of the Galaxy watching a stand-up show starring only Scottish comedians. You might be able to vaguely follow it, but you won't be laughing like everyone around you.

The other is that Jean-Claude van Damme is hardly in this film. I threw it on to review for this book project and watched eagerly to see what he'd get up to in a meta-Chinese comedy. Then I got sucked deeply enough into the picture that I was almost shocked when he showed up, at the very tail end of proceedings, playing the boss in the boss battle. Oh yeah, that's why I was watching! I'd completely forgotten!

That's because I got entirely caught up in the shenanigans of Da Peng, a fictional character played by Da Peng, the stage name of Dong Chengpeng, who also wrote and directed this film. He's playing himself in a similar way to how Van Damme played himself in JCVD, but he's a lot wackier, as you might expect from someone who started his movie career in a film called Radish Warrior. Many of the other actors here play themselves too, including some I recognise, like Eric Tsang, Sandra Ng and Ekin Cheng. Most are more than willing to send themselves up something rotten.

In this film, Da Peng is the star of a web TV show called Diors Man. There's a red carpet where he's going. People wave flags with his name on them. He knows how to play the crowd. As you might expect from all that, he also has a girlfriend with expensive tastes. She's Amber Kuo, played by Amber Kuo. He wants to propose. She wants a thirteen-million-dollar wedding ring. And that prompts him to talk with Wang Hai, a gangster boss with a fondness for movies strong enough that he's happy to give Da Peng ten million dollars to make one.

You already know this isn't going to end well, but it takes a quick dive into the crapper. One bizarre disgrace later and Da Peng is without a job, because he's promptly fired; without that thirteen-million-dollar ring, because he's lost it; and without a girlfriend, because she's out of the loser's life like shit through a goose. Oh, and Wang wants his money back and gangster bosses are pretty experienced in getting money back. Clearly, it's time for some sort of scheme.

Somehow, that scheme becomes Da Peng making a "Chinese super-realistic legendary action, romance, science fiction comedy." It'll be adapted from a comic book he wrote when he was a picked-on kid about A Li, from the Sagittarius planet, who becomes a superhero called Jian Bing Man, or Pancake Man, who takes on supervillains like Spicy Crayfish Man. It'll be shot by Whiskers, the paparazzo who's been shooting him for a year, using a "secret filming" technique. Oh, and that doesn't mean the technique is secret but that the people who are being filmed won't know they're being filmed. Oh yes, indeed.

For instance, award winning Hong Kong actress Sandra Ng is in town and the paparazzi group know where she goes jogging every night. So, they'll lie in wait, leap out to pretend to sexually assault her and escape with the footage of her reaction. It doesn't work, because they're inept, the camera battery's dead and, the next night, she's jogging with a hundred bodyguards, but it also doesn't work because Hong Kong actor Eric Tsang struggles along in her wake because he wants to be sexually assaulted by a superhero. Now look up the sexual assault allegations against him. This is very meta.

It's also very silly indeed. However, it has a surprising emotional depth too because we start to gain sympathy for Da Peng as he struggles against increasing odds to complete his film. He takes a job compering a wedding, only to get paid more to not compere that wedding. He starts MCing funerals for cash but ends up getting paid to drink instead. And, while Amber Kuo is clearly a gold digger he's best off without, he doesn't notice the gorgeous Yan Liu, played by the gorgeous Yan Liu, who's always there for him, even if it means driving a getaway vehicle so he can escape the cops.

I'd like to say that I wouldn't fail to see if someone like Yan Liu, who's still gorgeous even when making stupid faces, was in love with me, but I'm totally oblivious to that sort of thing too.

I learned a lot here. There are far more Chinese film stars than I've even heard of, and they all seem to have good humour. I learned how quickly they fall from grace and rise back to honour. I learned that I'm completely in lust with Yan Liu and googling the Yan Liu Bandage Dress only escalated that. I even learned some English as this weird Chinese superhero comedy Da Peng is making in this weird Chinese superhero comedy Da Peng made includes a lot of figurants and I had to look that word up. Apparently, they're just background extras.

And I learned that Jean-Claude van Damme could still do the splits in 2015. He enters the film doing the splits high on an industrial platform while wearing a villainous white suit. His fight with Da Peng involves more fighting than he did in the entirety of Swelter. And he gets the last line, kinda sorta out of meta. "Who is stronger?" Da Peng asks him. "Iron Man or me?"

"Iron Man never kicked my ass."

- Hal CF Astell

Pound of Flesh (2015)

3*Pound of Flesh*, released in 2015, is the Jean-Claude Van Damme film no one realized they were missing. It's unapologetic, and never once questions itself, in large part because of the fact that these characters, these actors, and the script are all in on what is happening. In so many ways this movie feels like a spiritual sequel to *Taken* in which Jean-Claude Van Damme plays the role of Liam Neeson while the role of the trafficked daughter, once played by Maggie Grace, is now Van Damme's kidney! When Deacon Lyle wakes in an icy bathtub in a fancy hotel in Manilla, it doesn't take him too long to follow the trickles of blood to his gore-soaked sheets, and then to a mirror where he notices that long scar where his kidney should be. Luckily, our protagonist has a very special set of skills as a "Kidnap and Rescue" expert, who now must rescue his own kidney.

Deacon cleans himself up, grabs the hotel Bible and begins to attempt to unravel what exactly happened him and why. With the help of an old friend, and with his distraught, estranged brother in tow, they hit a nightclub for answers. This is the moment this film wins its viewers over because not only does JCVD kick the crap out of a bunch of credit less thugs and he does so with that Bible! At this point *Pound of Flesh* starts to morph into a film of a bygone era, where fight scenes happen as regularly and seamlessly as a song and dance number might break out in a Gene Kelly film. And because everyone in this film buys in, there is a verisimilitude that never has you questioning any of it. This movie could have come out in 1995 and, likely, would have gotten a theatrical release. It fits right into the pantheon ofVan Damme films.

And it's not a comeback film for an aging action star; it doesn't do any of the things that a film does when it's winking at the camera or attempting to be clever. *Pound of Flesh* isn't trying to be cute when they reveal that

Van Damme isn't merely angry that his kidney was taken, but that it was intended to save the life of his dying niece. There is also no pause or wink when they tell you that Deacon is a match for his niece, but his brother is not a match for his own daughter. Everything in this film is part of the story they're telling. Even the villain, Drake, who has a lot of similarities to Bennet in *Commando*, doesn't feel over-the-top. I believe in a version of our world where prostitutes lure men to bed so that trained soldiers of fortune can traffic the victims' organs. I believe that underground fight clubs are normal.

When one can accept that the hyper-real is typical business, the ride is a lot of fun. It doesn't hurt that the movie is shot well and has high production value. It also has a lot of action! There are gunfights, there are martial arts fights, there are guys getting stabbed in the neck with bottles, car chases. At one point, JCVD strangles a guy in a car, while using one foot to pin the thug's gun hand to the side mirror while dragging his other leg into his famed splits! And from *Fight Club* to street fights, beating people with the Bible, and strangling them in cars, you are reminded that our hero has just had a kidney removed! And, still, it doesn't trip itself up over its own ridiculousness! One hopes, and assumes that like Liam Neeson, our hero will prevail, but like watching a wrestling match with Ric Flair, there are moments where we're not so sure.

As the search for his missing kidney continues, and with a number of bodies in his wake, Deacon adds Ana, the woman who set him up, to the crew. And in the quiet moments, the script, and our director, Ernie Barbarash, fill in some gaps and add some twists without it feeling like exposition. When we are told the backstory of why Deacon is a match and brother George is not, there is no real shock because no matter how convoluted things seem, the story is tight, it all checks out, and never feels like it's there to serve the story. And the story beats never seem like bridges to get you to the action. When we are told why it is that Ana was chosen for this operation, it seems so ridiculous, but like all of the previous things mentioned, it seems to all check out.

After an explosion disrupts our quiet moment of exposition and character building, our rag tag crew regroups, formulates their plan, and makes their final assault on the people who stole Deacon's kidney. There are explosions, hand to hand combat, and we even get a final confrontation between Deacon and Drake, a fight that has absolute unflinching consequences. And in this moment we get yet another twist that complicates our story and takes our action revenge flic to a place of moral dilemma. What happens if someone already has the kidney? A question that is asked several times along the journey, but now seeks an answer. Ultimately, nothing gets in the way of Deacon donating a kidney and still managing to do what is right! This movie delivers an atypical ending, and it all seems to check out as what would happen in the world of Deacon Lyle's Manilla.

With swagger and the confidence of a veteran action star, JCVD brings something to this overlooked action masterpiece that elevates it from the sort of thing one might find in late night syndication to something deserving of a time machine to deliver it to the decade where it belongs. A 90s classic that wasn't realized until decades later and under the radar, this movie is so much better than straight to video. In a world where kids stayed up late watching movies they shouldn't on HBO, this flic would have been a classic!

- Chris Brown

Jean-Claude Van Johnson (2016 – 17)

Directed by Peter Atencio (all six episodes), the series follows Jean-Claude Van Damme as he plays a fictional version of himself. It opens with him being retired from acting, and as we quickly find out, from a life as a secret agent. Van Damme clearly isn't happy in modern day L.A., and shortly after the pilot opens, he returns to his agent (Rashad) and tells her that wants back in.

She starts to try to book him a movie, when he tells her he wants back into the "other" thing as well. That's when viewers find out that she is also his handler. She places him on a movie, where he remains a bit fish out of water, but it's filming near where his assignment is. He's working with a former girlfriend and another agent who is to young remember JCVD's former career.

In the pilot of the series, Jean-Claude runs across Filip (also played by Van Damme), a fan who looks exactly like him, and who eventually comes to hate him after JCVD kills most of his friends. After exposing the drug lord he was sent to capture, JCVD realizes he's onto something bigger, only to uncover that one of the movie's producers, who is also a fan, is trying to build a weather control machine to take over the world.

Episodes:

Pilot (August 19, 2016)

What Year Do You Think This Is? (December 15, 2017)

A Little Conversation About Trust (December 15, 2017)

If You're Lucky (December 15, 2017)

Run to Nowhere (December 15, 2017)

The World Needs Its Hero (December 15, 2017)

The series ran for six episodes on Amazon Prime. It debuted in 2016 as part of a promotion where the pilot episode of several shows was produced, and viewers got to vote on their favorite to go to series. The other series produced were, The Tick and I Love Dick. Despite the original plan being to have people vote and the winning series getting produced, all three ended up getting made. I love Dick and Jean-Claude Van Johnson each got a single season, while The Tick ended up with two seasons.

It's cheesy, it's campy, and a little bad! That's what makes this show perfect. It's full of inside jokes, sight gags and very self-referential to JCVD's own career (especially *Timecop*). The series as a whole can be watched in an afternoon and the jokes, while funny the first time, land even better on a second viewing, especially the inside jokes that a viewer may miss the first time through.

It's great to watch JCVD making fun of himself (especially the *Timecop* jokes). The series does a really good job of keeping it light, while building to a well-deserved finale.

Other than *Timecop* (things are funny in threes, right?), this may be the best thing that JCVD has ever done.

I'm hoping for more seasons of something similar, maybe we find out that all of the 80s action heroes worked for this organization, and we get a season of each of them coming out of retirement. It's probably a pipe dream, but this show was so well written, it deserves more in any way that viewers can get it.

- Dave Herndon

Kickboxer: Vengeance (2016)

Not many of Van Damme's films have been remade. Honestly, I'm a bit surprised that not more of his classics have been given the option. Then again, there's probably a good reason as to why they have mostly been left in the 80s and 90s. However, if one movie had to be remade, Kickboxer has to be the one. Right?

There's no denying what they wanted to do when they remade this film. While I won't say this movie was supposed to make the viewer believe it could happen in real life, it did a great job of updating the timeline and really nailed making the movie more violent than the original. The violence ranges from physical fists to weapons while successfully attempting to recreate an 80s action movie with a modern-day twist.

There are many noticeable names sprinkled throughout the whole film that have played some role in the mixed martial arts world. Even the lead actor, Alain Moussi, has a martial arts background. However, the MMA presence does not take away from the film. The story is very identical to the original – two brothers travel to Thailand to face off against Tong Po. The scenes may be a little out of order from the original, but it does a good job in being its own movie while paying homage to the original. Alain Moussi is a decent Kurt Sloane while the late Darren Shahlavi plays a believable kickboxing champion in his brother, Eric. A big difference in this film compared to the original is that Eric gets killed by Tong Po rather than being paralyzed. This leads Kurt to avenge his brother's death, by any means necessary.

There are some great parts in this remake – seeing Kurt face off against Kavi (played by Georges St. Pierre), Dave "Batista" Bautista as Tong Po breaking stone pillars with his knees and elbows, and of course, Van Damme playing the role of the teacher. Seeing Van Damme in a reverse role like this was a very happy sight to see. He didn't try to steal the scenes from Alain but played well as a supporting actor.

As mentioned, Kurt plans on killing Tong Po for killing his brother. In the remake, Kurt initially decides he needs to kill Tong Po by shooting him while he's asleep. But everyone knows you can't kill Tong Po with a gun. As if he had superpowers, Tong Po notices the situation and points out to Kurt that his brother died a warrior while Kurt is nothing but a coward. Seeing Bautista as Tong Po was a great fit. The man is a naturally intimidating professional wrestler and he very much took this role seriously. He could have phoned it in but did the exact opposite, making his character even more intimidating than the original Tong Po.

The movie starts off a bit jumpy and may be a little difficult to follow as we don't truly know what's going on until about twelve minutes in the film. There's a flashback to Eric and Kurt and the start of their unfortunate misadventure. Gina Carano plays Marcia, a fight promoter that has ties to underground fighting in Thailand. Eric is convinced to go and fight his unknowingly last fight against the behemoth Tong Po. As Po breaks Eric's neck, the police raid the underground fight, causing spectators to scatter like cockroaches, leaving only Kurt with his brother's body.

Things get dicier as the movie unveils that certain officers are also corrupted by the underground fighting when Kurt is told to leave Thailand and never come back. Of course, he can't leave! Instead of getting on a plane, he finds himself reaching out to Master Durand to train him. JC seems reluctant but finally caves in after seeing the determination from Kurt. Throughout the film, we get some nice montages, Kurt falling in love with Officer Liu, Kurt beating opponents, and then finally getting the chance to face off against Tong Po.

One of the funnier scenes involves Master Durand and Kurt getting arrested by the police. They're arrested because Kurt is considered a fugitive and Master Durand is harboring said fugitive. They plan an escape that is fit for these type of films - JC plays the fool when a guard asks the whereabouts of Kurt. Cue the guard unlocking the door and Kurt coming down from the ceiling, taking him out. We get a great moment in the film as Michel Qissi (the original Tong Po) makes an appearance in the next cell. He questions out loud, "Hey, you forgot about me?" as the two leave.

- John Bruske

Kung Fu Panda 3 (2016)

After the reveal that Po's dad was still alive, as was an entire village of Pandas at the end of the second movie, the third picks up that storyline to finish the trilogy. Po, along with his adopted father, travel with his biological father back to the secret village of the pandas. Po's father lied to him about being a master of Chi in order to get him there, but it was because he was afraid Po would be defeated by Kai and killed.

Po in the meantime was struggling with being told he had to be the teacher at the Jade Palace and was happy to leave temporarily. Eventually Kai had stolen the Chi from every Kung Fu master and student in China other than Tigress, who escaped, and Po who was in hiding. Together, Tigress and Po train the village of pandas to use their unique skills to help fight Kai and attempt to save China.

Critically assessing the Van Dammage of the film, the character of Master Croc is mostly a non-speaking one in this movie. He only has one line before his Chi is stolen. Then Kai uses the Chi version of him (appearing as a green avatar) in the fight in the panda village, but none of the Chi's were in speaking roles.

Van Damme used his own voice, not a specially planned one for the line he spoke, much like in *Kung Fu Panda 2*. He did well with it, but it probably took longer to check his microphone, than to record his part in the movie.

- Dave Herndon

Kill 'Em All (2017)

Autumn Reeser's 2017 movie *Kill 'em All* — yeah, it's supposed to be Jean-Claude Van Damme's but it isn't — is fascinatingly broken.

It's not good, let me get that out there from the start, but it's certainly ambitious and some of it feels acutely refreshing. The rest feels like it was shot in modular fashion during COVID, as individual actors found themselves freed up from lockdowns and travel restrictions and the director stole a day to shoot a couple of their scenes with minimal crew. Except that wasn't the case, because this was released in 2017! So, it's fascinating but broken.

We're told from the outset that it's a revenge movie tied to the breakup of the former Yugoslavia and FBI agent Peter Stormare, for once not playing a Russian, later talks us through the political and socio-economic effects of that breakup in an infodump scene that we can safely skip. None of it matters. What matters is that JCVD's character, Phillip, is an action guy with a history and the question we're being asked is whether he's a good guy or a bad guy.

Initially, he's a patient, one who arrives at the Redondo Coast Medical Center in Los Angeles on a gurney, amidst a flurry of new patients on gurneys, so many that they quickly outnumber the staff at a hospital that's been abandoned, for no apparent reason, except for emergency operations. All the lights are on and it's well stocked, but the budget for extras obviously didn't extend past this single scene, because precious few other extras show up and few of them do anything except be blurs in the background. The film quickly focuses from this point into tiny groups of actors in tightly delineated scenes, like one nurse called Suzanne wheeling Phillip away for treatment or Radovan Brokowski showing up with a gun and shooting Dr. Todd dead.

While this sounds like the second half of *Hard Boiled* and we look forward to watching the whole place get destroyed during an epic shootout, that's what doesn't happen. The primary storyline is actually Suzanne being interrogated by the FBI and everything else unfolds in flashbacks, told from the perspective of one of the characters in this strangely corporate FBI office, all glass and brushed steel but without any decoration, except for a prominent photo of Lincoln on a cube wall in the background.

Many of these flashbacks are Suzanne's memories, which arguably could explain the lack of extras. Hey, it was traumatic! She just doesn't remember them. Others are extrapolations, based on little evidence because the FBI's computers are conveniently down, a crucial detail we completely fail to care about at the time. That's how we see JCVD's fights, because Suzanne wasn't there for most of them. They happen like a video game, level by level, and we learn who his opponents are first, with the sort of skimpy bios we see in character selection scenes. Who to fight today? How about Dušan, who met a random Asian with knives in a random corridor in L.A. six months ago and kicked his ass? Now, fight!

Oddly, given that the debuting director of this film, Peter Malota, is best known as a stuntman and fight coordinator, these fights are skimpy and disappointing. At least Dušan is played by Kris van Varenberg, JCVD's son and increasingly frequent co-star, who kicks high and fast but in a recognisable fashion. He moves well here, but he doesn't act. He's a highly trained mannequin and he's soon dead.

Better is Almira, a seductress/assassin who struts her stuff in Toronto in 2014. Mila Kalađurđević, unsurprisingly credited as Mila Kali, looks great and moves even better in a scene that's highly gratuitous but somehow features no nudity. She has serious moves, both sensuous and deadly. There's Ivan, who kills somebody in Moscow in 2008 so quickly that I blinked and missed it. And there's a pair of brothers, Radovan and Zoran, whom we see executing people in cold blood in Bosnia in 1999. The flashbacks set each of these bad guys up as ruthless and capable, so we can overestimate them when it's time for their fight scene with JCVD (or, in a couple of instances, Autumn Reeser, who isn't a martial artist). Oh, and all of them, including Phillip, are bodyguards for Klaus, who's therefore the super boss for the last fight.

The script, by three screenwriters with few prior credits, thinks that it's really clever but we're apparently supposed to believe that Zoran betrays Klaus and Phillip kills him, only for Klaus and his men to hunt down Phillip in the hospital. That makes no sense, but it makes us realise that the people telling us this story are unreliable narrators and we have no clue who's telling the truth or why they might not be. No spoilers, but there are a slew of twists coming to mess with our heads even more. I'm beginning to wonder if the adverts I suffered through on Plex were part of that, like the lady standing for Maricopa County attorney who's on Australia's front line. Erm, Arizona's front line?

That's a typical error for this movie, whose good bits are also bad bits. I liked that Phillip is seriously concussed, so has to fight bad guys with broken equilibrium. JCVD looks terrible in these scenes, but believably so and that does ratchet up the tension. However, being massively disorientated is the only way to explain his cringeworthy attempt to flirt with Suzanne. "You're the type of girl I would like to walk with you in the woods and listen to the birds," he suggests. "Plus, you're intelligent." We can tell that he knew how awful those lines are because we watch him actively cringe as he speaks them.

And maybe that explains the rest of this movie. It's overly complex, needlessly confusing as we yo-yo around time and with far more twists than it needs. But Autumn Reeser is excellent, even if her eventual wig isn't.

- Hal CF Astell

Kickboxer: Retaliation (2018)

How do you compete with *Kickboxer: Vengeance*? Trick question, you don't. *Kickboxer: Retaliation* doesn't even try to be a standard sequel. This movie is crazy. But in a good way. I wasn't expecting what I got when I watched this one. If I had to compare it to any of the original *Kickboxer* sequels, it makes about as much sense to the franchise as *Kickboxer 3*, featuring Sasha Mitchell.

Reprising his role as Kurt Sloane, Alain Moussi is back to kick some ass. But let's be honest, you're not reading an Alain Moussi book. That's right, Van Damme reprises his role as Durand, marking the first time he has ever appeared in a Kickboxer sequel. To add, we get even more famous names in the world of mixed martial arts, boxing, and cinema., with the biggest drawing power being Mike Tyson and Christopher Lambert. We also get the big bad antagonist, Hafthor Julius Bjornsson (aka the Mountain), playing Mongkut.

The movie immediately opens up with a foreshadowing dream sequence. As the credits role, images and clips of the original *Kickboxer* and *Kickboxer: Vengeance* play. Why? I think the better question is, why not? After *Kickboxer: Vengeance*, Kurt is now a popular MMA fighter. But even being famous isn't going to protect him from enemies in Thailand. After a brief talk with some U.S. Marshals, Kurt gets tasered and brought back to the land of Muay Thai.

Here, we meet Christopher Lambert in the role of Thomas Moore. Lambert does a great job of playing a slime ball steeped in corruption in Thailand. He has an offer – fight against the current champion, Mongkut. If Sloane wins, one million U.S. dollars, tax free. If he refuses, he goes to prison. What's an honorable man to do?

Kurt finds himself in prison among many crazy characters. The fight scenes that follow are enough to convince anyone to watch this film.

While Moore is trying to convince Kurt to fight, he still rejects the offer. We get a great introduction scene with Mike Tyson – Kurt gets into another fight and ends up interrupting Mike's meditation, which causes Mike to destroy Kurt but also start a friendship. Aw.

The movie is surprisingly well paced, especially with all of its training montages. It's through these montages that we meet some of the other characters, but more importantly, we get re-introduced to Master Durand! Durand is also in prison for his role in the death of Tong Po. But we can't just have normal Durand - Moore had him blinded for not giving up Kurt. It seems shocking but Durand says being blind has been a blessing. His other senses are heightened, and he knows the answers before the questions. Whatever that's supposed to mean.

To make the movie even crazier, Moore has Kurt's wife kidnapped. If he only did that in the beginning, he would have gotten Kurt to take the fight right away. The film is then filled with more training, Kurt getting his ass kicked further, and even a teaser fight between JCVD and Tyson, which made no sense except to please the fans.

For some reason, JC is allowed to see Mongkut train, but Moore's guys aren't worried as Durand is now blind. One of the funnier scenes happens when Mongkut receives an adrenaline cocktail in a comically large syringe while he plays a guitar looking more like a ukulele in his massive arms. After receiving the dose, he destroys two guys.

There's even more fan service when JC meets up with Lambert while he trains...with swords. Obviously, we now have to see both men fight each other with swords. Durand tries to convince Moore to replace him with Sloane in the fight but there's no chance.

During training, Kurt notices a certain tattoo that reminds him of the one in his dream. This starts the rescue sequence of the film. We get some more amazing fight choreography as Kurt is on a mission to save his wife.

This leads to him breaking into Moore's residence and having to immediately fight two ladies in bikinis. Yes, you read that correctly. We get a great old school martial arts fight scene trope – a room full of mirrors. While saving his wife and trying to make an escape, they bump into the biggest threat – Mongkut! During their battle, Liu tries to break it up but her interference leads to Mongkut accidentally delivering a giant blow that places her into a coma.

At the hospital, she wakes up and Kurt immediately tells her he needs to fight. She already knows. In order to win, Kurt needs to know Mongkut's weakness – a glass jaw. But it has to be perfectly timed when the monster's heart is racing.

Just as with the first film, the final fight takes place in a ridiculous setting – at an old Muay Thai temple. As expected, Kurt gets destroyed right away. I mean, bad. Worse than Tong Po. At the end of the round, instead of punching Kurt's face, Mongkut craters a stone statue next to Kurt's head. During the intermission, Mongkut gets his cocktail injection. It's round two with blades attached to knees and elbows. Kurt looks to be fairing better but it quickly ends as Mongkut delivers the pain. He kills Kurt with a double death blow. Seriously. A doctor comes in and checks. Liu can't believe it, so she grabs the adrenaline cocktail and jabs it into his chest. Kurt wakes up and we start getting the "White Warrior" chants. It's time for the final round.

Kurt takes in all of the advice from his trainers, gets blindfolded by Van Damme, and finally starts getting the upper hand. But right when it looks like he's about to win, Mongkut strikes the double sternum punch again. He then proceeds to drown Kurt in a shallow pool area. The past begins to play in Kurt's head – his brother, his doubt, his dream. It's not until he hears the words, "believe in yourself," that he begins to fight back. Van Damme shouts, "the kill shot!" as Kurt does a flash kick to Mongkut's jaw, knocking him down. He starts pummeling away until the big man grabs a loose blade and sticks it into Kurt. Kurt winces in pain but it's not enough to defeat him. He musters up the strength to wrap a chain around Mongkut's neck, choking him until he draws his final breathe. The end.

While this movie is ridiculously over the top, I still had a great time watching it. It definitely knew what it was going for and hit it out of the park. With all of the names associated to the project, its fast-paced action and incredible fight scenes, it is a must-watch for any martial arts movie fan. And once again, JCVD does it so well. There are rumors of a third film in the works. If true, I just hope Master Durand makes an appearance.

- John Bruske

Black Water (2018)

Back in the 1980's and '90's, the very concept of Arnold Schwarzenegger and Sylvester Stallone, the two biggest stars of not just the action genre, but arguably the entire movie industry, starring in the same movie together was nothing more than a pipe dream. There were large paydays and even larger egos at hand, so audiences would have to wait quite a long time (the 2010's to be exact) to see these pillars of testosterone-fueled cinema join forces.

Sadly, despite the abundance of action stars and martial artists that grew out of the 90's, having a film that paired two stars together was a bit of a rarity. The obvious outliers of course are 1992's *Universal Soldier* and 1993's *Demolition Man. Universal Soldier* is especially important to note as it treated action audiences to two action stars *in their prime* beating the hell out of each other for 95 glorious minutes. Granted, it wasn't the Austrian Oak and Italian Stallion in the leads, but producers were keen to the fact that if they couldn't get the A-list stars, they could go to that second rung and work with the B-List, i.e. Jean-Claude Van Damme and Dolph Lundgren. Some could even argue that Stallone himself was inspired by this gimmick with *Demolition Man*, and while he didn't square off against his Austrian counterpart, he also went down to the B-List and handpicked Wesley Snipes to square off against in 1993 (thus also still giving Sly the upper hand of sorts).

I only bring up the Schwarzenegger-Stallone comparison, because it parallels what was to come in *Black Water*. In 2013, Stallone and Schwarzenegger finally teamed up in a singular action film called *Escape Plan*. Granted, there were those *Expendables* movies, but some would argue that those don't entirely count due to the fact that in the first film, Arnold is more or less a fleeting cameo. In its sequel, *The Expendables 2*, Arnold has a longer role, however, he only shows up for a few scenes, and each one of his lines is an embarrassing callback to one of his earlier films. However, in *Escape Plan*, Stallone and Schwarzenegger star as inmates in a high-tech prison who must put aside their differences and team-up in order to escape. Yes, it's Arnold and Sly way past their prime and starring in a film that should have been made in 1993, however, despite its dopiness, as well as the fact that its two leads would realistically be retired on a golf course, it's still a fun callback to the action flicks of yesteryear.

Which finally brings me to *Black Water.* Considering that Arnold and Sly teamed up in a film past their prime, the direct-to-video market was also tapping into this same gimmick. And producers knew where to go, once again to the second rung and hiring Jean-Claude Van Damme and Dolph Lundgren. As evidenced in *Universal Soldier*, Van Damme and Lundgren have a fantastic chemistry, so it only made sense to put them back together in a film, but one where instead of beating the hell out of each other, they're now fighting *on the same side*. Yet despite the difference in casting, *Black Water* is essentially the same movie as *Escape Plan*. A buddy of mine coined it best – it's the Junior Varsity version of *Escape Plan*.

Let's run down the list of comparisons:

- In *Black Water*, Jean-Claude Van Damme is the Sylvester Stallone analog who finds himself wrongfully locked up in a prison.
- Dolph Lundgren is the Arnold Schwarzenegger analog where they both play seasoned inmates with knowledge of the prison who assist the leads in escaping.
- Both films take place in prisons that exist off the grid; *Escape Plan*, it's a high-tech facility that sits in the middle of the ocean where the prison guards all inexplicably wear masks. In *Black Water*, things are a little more scaled back to assist the much lower budget, so we get a submarine setting… a standard trope of these direct-to-video films.
- Black Water also has some fun in-jokes that anyone who is familiar with the career of Jean-Claude Van Damme (i.e. "The Muscles from Brussels") will get a kick out of. For one, Patrick Kilpatrick (familiar

to fans as "The Sandman" from *Death Warrant*) shows up as the villain; he also gets to repeat his classic "Welcome to Hell!" line that I'm convinced is a callback.

Yet despite this keen bit of casting, how does *Black Water* stack up as not just an action movie, but as the JCVD-Lundgren reunion we hoped for? Let's just say that it falls short of what I was hoping for. When I first got wind of this film when it was in production, I envisioned a *Lethal Weapon* or *Tango & Cash* of sorts… I wanted to see these two tough guys trading barbs, then high fiving one another after they mow down an army of commandos. And there's a very brief moment at the end where they do team-up, JCVD winks at Lundgren, and you think that it was all worth it. Sadly, after one battle, Dolph inexplicably leaves not just the action, but also the film, leaving Van Damme to pick up the slack and finish the movie.

The rest of the film is standard cliched tropes of DTV action films… We get turncoat CIA operatives and a flash drive, which is used to drive the plot. In case you're curious, the flash drive contains the identities of every CIA agent, including the dirty ones… you know the rest.

Regarding JCVD and Dolph, they're okay in the film. Dolph is actually the standout; you can tell that he's having tons of fun in his minimal role. As for Van Damme… Well, his acting is okay, despite the fact that he's resorting to the MO that he's applied for the past ten years of his career – sullen, morose, quiet. Gone is that goofy charm he exhibited in his prime when he was on *The Arsenio Hall* show plugging *Double Impact*. Although, considering his face is significantly older and weathered with stories to tell, some could argue that he's leaning into his appearance with these roles.

In the end, the film isn't necessarily terrible. And compared to much of the low-budget dreck that's permeating the DTV market these days, it's actually a breath of fresh air. In short, streaming has essentially decimated the market resulting in shrinking budgets, which in turn results in limited sets, shooting days, etc. So on that front, *Black Water* is a success.

But as a fan of both these guys, the film still leaves you wanting just a little more. It doesn't give the same kind of impact that *Universal Soldier* did back in 1992. Then again, that was also over 30 years ago, and both JCVD and Dolph have aged considerably since then; they simply don't have the same physical prowess that they once did. So perhaps I'm just being nostalgic, wanting something that just isn't possible in this day and age. Oh well. I can also imagine what a *Black Water* might have been. And it wouldn't have been a carbon copy of a film starring two guys from that 90's A-List.

- Sean Malloy

The Bouncer (2018)

Regardless of your opinion on the earliest Van Damme films, his later output has found him to be a compelling presence in a series of fascinating roles. It turns out that world weary Van Damme has an endearing vulnerability and is so easy to root for as a protagonist.

The Bouncer is a French-Belgian film by director Julien Leclerq, and it continues the new tradition of JCVD films in which he has aged into a super appealing action star. The plot is whatever, almost a standard action-y trope in a lot of ways, but there is a freshness to the whole thing because, frankly, Van Damme evolved into a pretty damn good actor somewhere along the way.

Lukas (Van Damme) the bouncer accidentally injures a patron at the establishment where he, um, bounces, and as it turns out, the guy (who really sort of did the whole thing to himself; Lukas didn't even throw a punch) is the son of a member of Parliament. This turns into Lukas having to protect/save his daughter from a strange "kidnapping" in which Lukas is forced to work undercover at a strip joint whose owner is printing counterfeit money.

So yeah…a lot of…stuff.

There's more here, including a botched attempt at trading a crack cocaine cook for counterfeit bills, but it's all kind of strange and even a bit anticlimactic in several ways. The resolution of his daughter's danger sorta happens midway through the movie and that doesn't even feel like a spoiler for the film's ending.

But to be honest…overall, THIS IS A PRETTY GOOD MOVIE. I had to put it that way, because I was expecting some bland, low budget looking affair, and this is not that. It's a totally watchable (at times even absorbing) foray into a modern sort of action flick, particularly in light of the stuff that Stallone now does; a retrospective in a way…a rebirth for a protagonist who has had the more eventful amount of his action happen *prior* to the point where we are dropped into in the films. Sort of the "last hurrah" of a character that already existed prior to their standalone movie.

It works, it's effective, and while Van Damme does get to participate in a satisfying amount of pretty well choreographed fight scenes (including one that might count as one of the worst job interviews ever committed to film), there is a lot of goodness here besides the fighting to recommend. It's actually quite touching, and the relationship between Lukas and his daughter is realistic and does a lot to get us into the position for some sort of emotional payoff.

The movie tells a complete story of an interesting fella with a strong cast of side characters. Several other figures aside from Lukas have grounded, three dimensional stories behind their inclusions, and watching Lukas interact with them is fulfilling in an unexpected way.

The whole thing is shot really well, and the narrative is easy to follow (even when the convoluted plot gives us a lot to remember), since we are able to pick up on what Lukas has to do next from event to event. It's never a boring watch, and our hero exudes a sort of earned, determined attitude from moment one.

And really, isn't that all we can ask for of a modern Jean Claude outing?

- Paul Counelis

We Die Young (2019)

I'm going to start out this essay by owning up to the fact that it was initially hard to write. I submitted essays for the previously released collections *Hard to Watch* and *Missing the Action*, and both essays were significantly easier to write. For *Hard to Watch*, the movie I watched was so ridiculously terrible and Steven Seagal is such a human cartoon that I had loads to talk about. For *Missing the Action*, I was asked to write about the theme songs to *Walker, Texas Ranger*, a brain-dead TV show whose star sang the theme song (almost always a terrible idea). But I don't have any particularly strong feelings about Jean-Claude Van Damme, and I was concerned that I wouldn't have anything to write about. But as it turns out this was the perfect movie for me, or anyone else who is ambivalent about JCVD, to watch and write about because it seems like the makers of the movie were pretty ambivalent about him too.

JCVD is the most recognizable name on the list of credits by far but in this tale of MS13 gangsters and spoiled youth he manages to be both essential to the plot while being the least interesting character on the screen at all times. He plays Daniel, an Afghanistan War vet living in a poor area of Washington D.C. controlled by MS13 gangs. And he doesn't speak - he has an injury from an IED, and it's heavily implied that he has a vent in his throat even though it's hidden behind a handkerchief. Daniel is also addicted to Vicodin, which he purchases from a 14-year-old named Lucas, a junior member of the ruling gang in Daniel's part of the city. With all of this character detail and a rich back story revealed throughout the movie, you'd think this character would grab your attention more. And yet, most of the time that he's on-screen he's just kind of *there*. No emotions, nothing to engage with, just *present*.

The movie was really enjoyable as a whole. The actors, straight-from-Central-Casting, chew the scenery. The filmmakers indulge in some semi-subtle steals from The Godfather franchise, and you even see some surprisingly graphic scenes; one of a bunch of gangsters beating the shit out of Lucas's 10-year-old brother Miguel, the other of the unfortunate and gory demise of Lucas and Miguel's dog. Is it a *great* movie? It is not. But it was reasonably entertaining for a direct-to-video mid-budget thriller. Caveat emptor, though. If you're a rabid fan of JCVD, you'll probably be disappointed. JCVD grimaces and plods through the role like he was channeling Clint Eastwood in *Gran Torino*. There are a few fight scenes where it feels like he sneaks in a couple of his action-star moves. But mostly, he grimaces and schlumps around. Can I give two shrugs instead of two thumbs up?

- Daryl Bean

Counterpoint: It amazingly never felt like a cartoon or that the shooters didn't have good aim. It suited the danger of the elements that the boys were in and thus suited the plot. The flashbacks to the war are also quick and are more to show Jean Claude's mindset in lieu of his action abilities. He spends more time trying to avoid fighting those around him as opposed to wanting to kick everyone's ass. It's the definition of being cast against type.

The final shoot out is a bloody mess, but when you deal with drugs and drug busts, it's bound to happen. It's more than a shoot-out, it's an all-out war and it really makes the audience realize how dire the circumstances are for the characters to choose that way of life. It is filled with just as much sadness and heartbreak as it is with bullets and blood, we care about the characters and the struggles. It also deals with power struggles rising to the top of whatever chain you are a part of, and everything trying to bring you down. It's a movie to watch because of the themes and I hesitate to call it a "guy's" movie; it has a real story with a real message and it conveys it with conviction. The title may seem suited for Steven Seagal going on a rampage, but when you think about what it conveys and what the character's go through and the actions they have to take, I couldn't think of a better title, and I highly recommend it.

- Stephen Kessen

The Last Mercenary (2021)

Is it good? Hell no! But it *is* entertaining.

The movie, which is in French and then dubbed over without a single attempt to match lip movements, or even approximate length of speech, has several fun moments. One of those is due to the dubbing, since star Jean-Claude Van Damme speaks English, he did his own dubbing, and still didn't manage to match his mouth movements.

The movie opens on a man being held captive, bag over his head, a few seconds later, we see Van Damme, in his signature splits, holding himself up in the rafters of this building. He's undercover, though we don't know that at the time. Had he stayed in this outfit the whole movie, it might have fit better, as he was playing an older bearded man. At that point, I thought the movie was being set up well. A *Lethal Weapon*-style "I'm too old for this shit" last mission of sorts which is fitting since JCVD was 61 years old when filming this.

Regardless of that preferred conceit, the next time we see him, he is "younged down," if you will, back to looking like he normally does, followed by a scene of him completely de-aged and set in the 1990s. It is apparent the filmmakers spent most of the CGI budget for the movie on this one element.

The entirety of the movie is about a man, a retired "legendary" secret agent Richard 'The Mist' Brumere (Van Damme), who comes out of hiding to help his estranged son, Archibald (Samir Decazza) out of a jam. This son, whom he had never met, was given lifetime immunity for any crime, and a monthly allowance, in exchange for Van Damme's character disappearing forever. 'The Mist' takes the deal thinking he has set Archibald up and protected him from the life of a womanizing, action-centric super spy father that could bring him nothing but danger and misery.

Flash forward more than 20 years, the adult son is with a friend buying marijuana in France when his bank card stops working. This is what kicks off the events of the film. In a bureaucratic nightmare scenario, a useless government worker accidentally canceled the son's allowance which triggers agents tracking down Archibald, now confused with a dastardly arms dealer, and caused his caretaker to be murdered. It is then left up to Brumere to rescue his son. The son's identity had been used in gun trafficking, and with the allowance canceled, so was the immunity.

Billed as an "action comedy," the movie works better if one looks at it straight up as a comedy. The action scenes are often mis-timed, and poorly filmed, making them come off as inauthentic. There are some intriguing concepts here, though. A great deal of Van Damme's recent work tends to be self-referential, at times an homage to his past work and other times as a parody. *The Last Mercenary* functions the same way, most notably in the recognition given to Van Damme's, arguably, most popular film *Bloodsport* (it is, after all, the namesake film for the volume you are currently reading).

To that end, Van Damme's character appears almost as a quick-change artist at times, which is made easy with movie magic, but appears in several different costumes throughout the movie. This is where the debate in the film lies. Is this an example, utilizing dynamic of costuming, of the Van Damme character being the suave super-agent with the ability to adapt to any scenario and even keeping his identity secret from Archibald, or is it simply a way to 'show off' in a filmic sense? I would err on it being a deliberate show of filmmaking prowess and awareness separating *The Last Mercenary* from the fast-paced actioners of Van Damme's youth and into the thoughtful, reflective phase he is currently in. As a conclusion to that bit of storytelling, for most of the narrative, Brumere keeps his identity secret from his son, but as the third act kicks off, another bumbling government official lets the secret slip, causing a disagreement between the two. In this scene, one could make the argument that Archibald calling his father a coward and exiting is akin Van Damme himself exorcising the folly of youth and realizing that this type of thoughtful approach could be synchronous with non-stop action. Possibly, Brumere is as regretful of missing that time with Archibald as Van Damme is of missing the past few decades to create thoughtful action cinema.

Or all of that is just claptrap and The Last Mercenary, as the last entry in *Bloodspurt*, needed a send-off worthy of Van Damme as auteur.

Overall, *The Last Mercenary* is a worthy addition the Van Damme oeuvre but does suffer mightily from a lack of budget. Of course, with the necessity for Brumere to be older this particular film could never have been made by a younger Van Damme in the same role, but if it were given the budgetary and cinematic advantages of some of those older films it may have been received far more warmly.

- Dave Herndon

Minions: The Rise of Gru (2022)

As an addendum to this exhaustive volume, Jean Claude Van Damme most certainly has a large body of work that has surpassed thirty-five years of cinema gold. It's rare though, that you will find an appearance of the "Muscles from Brussels" in a big budget family film. 2022's release of *Minions: The Rise of Gru* is one of those rare, unique additions to JCVD's resume. Amazingly enough, our noted action hero extraordinaire knocks his silly voice-over contribution out of the park. In *Rise of Gru* he plays Jean Clawed, one component of the devious supervillain team known as the Vicious 6, curiously without those aforementioned muscles, but sporting one hand that ends in an oversized lobster claw. A collection of the greatest baddies of the time, the Vicious 6 is experiencing some difficulties as the members boot out their long-time leader, Wild Knuckles (Alan Arkin). Comedy ensues, including Minions farting, among other assorted hijinks (and, yes, that stands out due to my pubescent sense of humor) through its 90 minute run-time. Aside from Steven Carell as hour "hero" Gru, Van Damme puts forth the sharpest and funniest voice-over in the film. It is self-referential, like a great deal of Van Damme's later work, and really plays into the meta vibes of the Minions universe. If you are a true fan of Van Damme, you must take in this rare non-action addition to his repertoire. If you are not a true fan of Van Damme, then why did you even buy this book?

- Jeff Dolniak

The Authors

Jon Arking *(aka Jon King)* is a Michigan-based broadcaster and journalist with over 35 years of experience. He has authored two children's books, *Ishkadoodle: A Boy, His Vacuum & Their Outerspace Adventure* and *Ishkadoodle & The 8 Planets of Hanukkah*. He is also the co-author of *Hot Mess* and the upcoming *Grounds*.

Hal CF Astell is an award-winning author, critic, publisher and film festival director who runs the Apocalypse Later Empire from his lair in Phoenix, AZ. He has seven books in print through Apocalypse Later Press and a few million words online at *Apocalypse Later Reviews*, which celebrated its fifteenth anniversary in 2021. The Apocalypse Later International Fantastic Film Festival (ALIFFF) is in its sixth year. He brings quality films to new eyeballs at conventions across the southwest through the Apocalypse Later Roadshow. His website is apocalypselaterempire.com.

Daryl Bean lives, works, and does things in relative anonymity and is totally fine with that. He'd put his website address here, but he doesn't have one.

Kurt "Thunderlord" Belcher lives in the mythical kingdom of Kentucky. He must continually dodge Bloody Thraborlaxes and Golden Shlob Bœars to make his way to the market at Neckboneton to sell his ridiculous paper scribbles. He likes dogs.

Chris Brown is a longtime film fan and budding action movie star. He is the proprietor of Comics and More in Madison Heights, MI.

John Bruske is a co-host to many podcasts, including the *Jean Pod Van Dammecast*, *Rage in a Cage*, and *Everyday I'm Russellin'*. When not trying to completely watch the Canon Films filmography, he spends time with his family and working on intellectual properties.

Michael Cieslak is a lifetime reader and writer of horror, mystery, and speculative fiction. He is an officer in the Great Lakes Association of Horror Writers and is the editor of the *Erie Tales* anthologies. His works have appeared in a number of collections including *DOA: Extreme Horror, Dead Science, Vicious Verses and Reanimated Rhymes*, the GLAHW anthologies, *Alter Egos* Vol 1., and the collaborative steampunk novel *Army of Brass. Urbane Decay*, a collection of Michael's short fiction, was released in 2018 by Source Point Press. Michael is the Editor in Chief of Dragon's Roost Press and his mental excreta, including his personal blog *They Napalmed My Shrubbery This Morning*, can be found on-line at thedragonsroost.net.

Paul Counelis is a freelance writer (*Rue Morgue, Scary Monsters, Fear Finder, Fright Times*), author (*Evil World Outside, 25 Underrated Horror Films and 'The Exorcist', The Greatest Horror Movie Ever Made*) and member of the Flint Horror Collective hailing from urban, renegade Flint, Michigan. As Uncle Salem he is the voice of horror punks Lords of October and the host of a weekly online radio show, *Blank Generation with Uncle Salem.*

Justine Defever currently resides in Michigan and is an Associate Professor of English and Communications at Cleary University. Her poetry has been recently featured in *Poets' Choice, Sad Girls Club Literary Blog, Silent Spark Press,* and *Wingless Dreamer.* In addition to her publication schedule, Justine placed in the 2022 Ekphrastic Poetry Contest at the Muskegon Museum of Art. During July 2022, Justine completed a residency in Edinburgh, Scotland while finishing an MFA in Creative Writing at Arcadia University.

Jeff Dolniak is an enigma wrapped in a damp hanky. Over the past 45 years, Jeff has strived for mediocrity with acting roles in cult films such as *Blown, Desert Man Beast* and *Sportkill.* Cult film aficionados may also know him as the creator of the popular DVD series, *42nd Street Forever.* Currently he churns out news and reviews for Cinema Head Cheese.

Ron Ford is an actor, writer and filmmaker from the Seattle area. In 1994, after moving to LA, he sold his first screenplay, which became the horror hit, *The Fear.* He became a filmmaker in 1997 with his directorial debut, *Alien Force*, starring Burt Ward of Batman fame. He became a gun for hire for film distributors, who could be relied upon to deliver salable movies on budget and on schedule. He produced, wrote and directed more than a dozen genre titles, including *Hollywood Mortuary, Tiki, Mark of Dracula* and *Witchcraft XI: Sisters in Blood*. As an actor, he can be seen in the movies *Home of the Brave, Killer Tomatoes Eat France*, and many others, as well as on the TV shows *Z Nation, The Young Riders, Two Busy Debras* and *Hey, Dude.* In 2003 he moved to Spokane, WA where he continues to live and work.

Erik Gutierrez is a Detroit born and raised self-taught artist-writer, and comic book creator (*Max the Inebriated Rabbit*) who wrote his first feature film *Bender*, which is streaming on Amazon Prime and Tubi. He's also a rabid film geek who can talk anything from the most obscure film to the most mainstream dreck out there.

David C. Hayes is an author, performer, filmmaker and academic. Visit him online at www.davidchayes.com.

Dave Herndon is a pretty simple man. He runs a newspaper in his day job, and does many creative things "on the side," in his spare time, including writing and editing comic books and stories, designing enamel pins and iron-on patches and much more. He owns the vending business Turtle Trinkets and generally just likes to enjoy life... and pizza!

Kent Hill is **a** screenwriter, author, publisher and podcaster. First published in the United States in 2013 by StrangeHouse Books, Hill would go on to write numerous novellas and short stories published individually and in a variety of anthologies. He currently has screenplays in development and is a writer of upcoming films from Rene Perez at www.thedarkestmachines.com. He lives on 'The Downs' in Queensland, Australia with his wife and son.

Pat Kawula is a writer, editor, and curator of the award-winning comic anthology *Get in the Game* published by Source Point Press. When he is not hiding under his desk suffering from an incurable case of Imposter Syndrome, he will peek out to write something witty. This bio is NOT one of those times... although maybe it is. Who knows?

Stephen Kessen was born July of 1989 in Cincinnati Ohio. He recently earned his master's degree from Regent University with a focus on Directing and Producing. He writes screenplays, directs movies, and acts with his film *Moving Ashley* winning over a dozen awards from various festivals across the world. When he's not working in the performing arts, he can be found reading murder mystery novels, traveling, and playing with his two cats, Chloe and Tybalt. A ravenous reader from a young age.

Stan Konopka had found his home in the pages of books. Being able to feel and live the stories of other people eventually lead him down the dark and lonely path to becoming a writer. Now consumed by the very words he once loved a writer he had become. With the hit three-part series, *The Rejected* from Source Point Press, he claimed his place in the world of the written word.

Joe LaLonde is an award-winning blogger who loves to combine his love for movies and his desire to see people grow their leadership abilities. He writes about leadership at https://jmlalonde.com and has released a book titled *Reel Leadership* which can be found wherever books are sold.

Sean Malloy was proudly raised on a healthy diet of action cinema from the 80's and '90's. He has since used his love of the glory days of action films to start his podcast, *"I Must Break" This Podcast*, which examines the career of fellow action star, Dolph Lundgren. When he's not discussing or expounding upon his love of these films, Sean is a family man who enjoys spending time with his wife, two children, and dog. And yes, he has already started exposing his children to the very same films he grew up watching.

Kevin Moyers is an author and podcaster who feels fully vindicated in choosing Jean-Claude Van Damme in the "Who would win a fight?" argument way back in the 1990s.

Andrew J. Rausch is a film journalist and the author of more than fifty books. This includes such titles as *The Cinematic Misadventures of Ed Wood* (w/ Charles E. Pratt Jr.), *The Films of Martin Scorsese and Robert De Niro*, and *My Best Friend's Birthday: The Making of a Quentin Tarantino Film*. He writes for numerous publications and is an online editor for *Diabolique* magazine. He lives with his wife and children in Independence, Kansas.

Jed Rowen is an actor living in Los Angeles who would happily volunteer to get kicked in the face by JCVD.

A P Sessler, a resident of North Carolina's Outer Banks, wishes he could stick to walls and jump trees without the aid of wires while fighting 50 bad guys at once. His all-time favorite martial arts film is the Shaw Brothers' *Five Elements Ninjas* aka *Chinese Super Ninjas*.

Montilee Stormer is a horror writer, film reviewer, and podcaster who never expected to actually live the inescapable horror of a Steven Segal movie. She now silently weeps for what could have been, but feel free to Google her name and despair along with her.

William Tea doesn't know aikido, but he does know how to write scary stories, as well as the occasional cult film review. Stalk him online at williamtea.com.

David Ullman is a filmmaker, musician, and podcaster from Northeast Ohio. He lives in Northfield, Minnesota with his wife and two dogs. More at www.davidullman.net.

Tony Doug Wright is a writer of comics and a graphic novel for Source Point Press. He's a husband, father, historian, lost soul of rock and roll, and a true crime writer.

www.ingramcontent.com/pod-product-compliance
Ingram Content Group UK Ltd.
Pitfield, Milton Keynes, MK11 3LW, UK
UKHW021907190726
13853UKWH00002B/560

9 798887 710808